FUN in the SON

FUN in the SON

How to Stay Young All Your Life

Larry D. Sledge

iUniverse, Inc.
Bloomington

FUN in the SON
How to Stay Young All Your Life

iUniverse books may be ordered through booksellers or by contacting:

iUniverse
1663 Liberty Drive
Bloomington, IN 47403
www.iuniverse.com
1-800-Authors (1-800-288-4677)

ISBN: 978-1-4620-2695-1 (sc)
ISBN: 978-1-4620-2696-8 (hc)
ISBN: 978-1-4620-2697-5 (ebk)

Printed in the United States of America

iUniverse rev. date: 07/20/2011

CONTENTS

Dedicated to my wife, Louise . . .

a *DAISY* in

a world filled with

Dandelions!

FOREWORD

By being the son of Larry and Louise Sledge, I have had their leadership and guidance all my life. They have touched the hearts of many other young people through the years of their ministry. At Baptist institutions such as Ridgecrest and Fort Caswell, church retreats and camps, and many other places, they have sought to bring God's Word to teen-agers.

The pages that follow describe actual experiences with young people that have stepped into the Sledge's lives. Christian fellowship is probably one of the major necessities in a teenager's life. Many young people have come and gone from these functions through the years, and I believe all of them were touched in some way by the spiritual atmosphere within these surroundings.

I only hope that other young people (and Adults) will find as much joy and happiness through Christian fellowship as I and the people described in this book have found.

In God's love,
Brian D. Sledge

Being the younger of Larry and Louise's two children, I didn't always understand exactly what my Mom and Dad did. I often thought of the group retreats at Ridgecrest, church camps, etc. as just a bunch of kids all getting together. As I grew up, I saw those kids turn to teenagers and those teenagers turn to young adults and those young adults turn into the men and women they are today. It was then I finally realized that through the love and faith of my parents, they have had such an impact on so many lives.

There was a plaque that hung in our home that said everything my parents stand for . . . It said, "Don't Give Up On Me; God's Not Finished With Me Yet" . . . It didn't matter what side of the tracks you came from, or the color of your skin, or the troubles you may have had; since God loved you and He wasn't giving up on you, then neither would my Mom and Dad. They have opened our home and their hearts to so many, and if they could guide only *one* then it was well worth everything.

I, myself, look back and realize that with the organized structure of us teenagers getting together, and with all the love anyone could ever ask for, I have been changed and become the woman I am today. This book tells of many other lives and how they also came to be changed throughout the years. I just hope you enjoy reading it as much as I and so many others enjoyed experiencing it. I pray it also will touch you and bring you closer to God.

In His love,
Tamela M. Sledge Hunt

INTRODUCTION

Someone has said that, "Youth is not a matter of age, but rather, a state of mind." . . . It is for that reason I have sought to write a book to be enjoyed by youth of all ages—from thirteen to one hundred! Some of us have just been young *longer* than others! I have known some who were *old* at seventeen and others who stayed *young* in their eighties.

My wife and I hope to stay young the rest of our lives, and one of the best ways we have found to keep a youthful view of life is to invest time with young people. Notice I said "invest", not "spend", as time with youth is an investment in the future, not something that is "spent" and all gone. Over the years God has given us many opportunities to be with youth in several churches and in differing communities.

I actually began Youth work while still a teen-ager myself. Our Sunday School teacher drove a long-distance truck and was away occasionally on Sundays, so I was asked to be the assistant teacher at the age of seventeen. I was influenced by many people during my early years—parents who reared me in a Christian home, Vacation Bible School workers who took time to be interested in me as an individual, and a dedicated Scoutmaster who cared enough to encourage me to accept Christ at the age of twelve. But it was not until years later that I realized how much two other people had influenced my life.

I grew up in a small church that had no staff other than a pastor, and there was no organized ministry to youth in the church. Although I sang in the choir, was active in Sunday School and Baptist Training Union, and attended every special activity anytime the church doors opened, I remember very little of what took place inside the church building. When I think of those years, I most often think of the good times we had in the back yard of our Training Union leaders.

This couple had three sons of their own; who were either married or away in service, but their home was always open at any hour to the young people of the community. There were few girls I ever dated who didn't go with me to their home at one time or another. Many were the times my friend Billy Slate and I double-dated and went by their home on Sunday afternoons.

Youth fellowships consisted of popcorn and cokes as we played checkers or listened to phonograph records in their living room. We never needed an invitation—the "gang" just seemed to gather there. How often the Farmers must have had other plans but were willing to change them in order to listen to us and provide a wholesome environment where we could be ourselves.

My wife, Louise, and I were married shortly after high school graduation and one of our basic philosophies regarding the establishment of a home was that we would welcome young people through our doors at any time of the day or night. Although it has caused loss of sleep and last-minute changes of our plans, we have been blessed with witnessing and counseling opportunities which would never have been possible otherwise.

Over the years we have sought to accept all youth as *persons* without always approving their *actions*. I do not believe we can force our doctrinal beliefs or personal code of ethics and morality on them. We must lead them to discover for themselves. So often adults tend to search the scriptures *for* our teens and then *tell* them what *we* found. This is not the example the apostle Paul left for us in the New Testament. In Acts 17:11, it is evident that he had encouraged the Berean Christians to dig, search, and explore the scriptures for themselves. I believe Bible truths discovered, or moral and ethical convictions reached first-hand, will do more to prepare young people for the day when parents and teachers are not around to make decisions for them! I believe a consistent, committed Christian life lived before our youth will do more to lead them spiritually than insisting that they "buckle under" to our way of thinking simple because "we are older and have more experience".

Before any effective work can be done with Youth, a person has to win their respect and confidence. This is not automatic; it does not come merely because a person has been called or elected to work with them. It is not to be expected just because a leader is older than those with whom he or she works. A breakthrough at this point can only come after considerable exposure to teenagers. A retreat or similar "get away" activity where the leader "lives with" the teens allows them to see both the leader's strong and weak points and learn that the leader is human too. My wife and I have had many hours of fun and fellowship together with scores of young people as well as experiencing those serious moments when great decisions have been made in the very presence of God. Whether in the prayer garden at Ridgecrest, the seashore of Fort Caswell, the dining room at Camp Forest, or in the privacy of our living room or den, we have seen young people grow spiritually in their relationships to God and to other youth. As they have been left free to be themselves—even with the freedom to make mistakes, they have grown at their own unique pace and in God's own time. We have discovered together that truly there is . . . Fun in the Son!

May the reading of these pages help you to see real Christianity—not as a negative approach to life but as a joyous celebration! To that end we open our hearts to share with you these personal vignettes which have formed our spiritual diary over the years.

WHERE IT ALL BEGAN

On June 15,1936, a baby boy was born to Roscoe and Leola Sledge in a basement apartment at 917 Redding Street in High Point, North Carolina. These were the days doctors still made house calls, and Dr. J.W. Slate had come that evening after a long day at his clinic. As the evening wore on, he said, "I'm really tired; is there some place where I could lie down for few minutes?" A folding canvas Army cot was set up and he was able to get some rest until about 12:30 in the morning. After the baby arrived, the new parents were only charged $25 for the doctor's services!

Roscoe was employed at Adams-Millis hosiery mill and Leola had previously moved to High Point with three of her sisters from their father's tobacco farm in Surry County. She also had worked for a different hosiery mill, but never worked outside the home after the baby was born. The child was named Larry Dale Sledge—the middle name in honor of Joe Dale, an Adams-Millis plant superintendent, who was a respected work associate and personal friend of the Sledges. Larry had to explain to schoolteachers for years that his name was not a nickname for "Lawrence", as only "Larry" was shown on his birth certificate. You now know how this writer came into this world and began the journey that has resulted in this book being published at his age of 75!

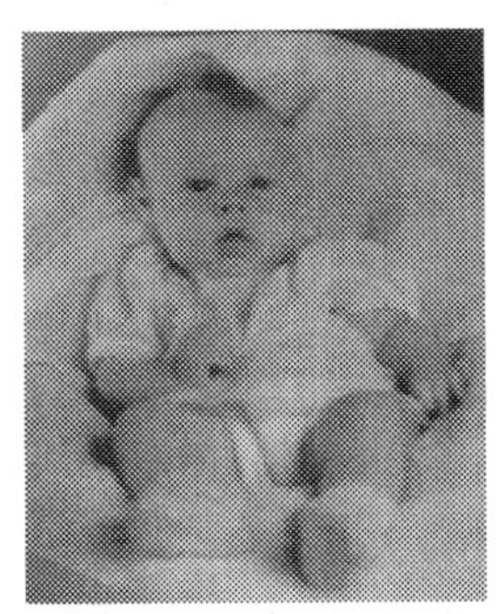

"It's a Boy!"

CHILDHOOD YEARS

My parents left that small basement apartment, and we lived for a time with my grandmother, Lizzie Spradley, on Ward Street in High Point. They later bought a lot and built a small four room clapboard house on a rural dirt road south of town.

As the city grew and gained a reputation as the Furniture Capital of the South, the city limits were extended and streets on the rural mail routes were given names. Franklin D. Roosevelt had won a second term as U.S. president in 1936, so our street became "Fala Street", in honor of the president's dog! That's where I lived until the time of our marriage in 1955.

My parents always had a vegetable garden, a large grape arbor, and a number of chickens in the backyard. Since there were no other houses nearby, they also raised two pigs every year in the edge of a wooded area some distance from the house. Mother cooked on a wood-burning cook-stove and sewed most of her dresses from *chicken feed sacks* that were decorated with flowers and pretty designs in those days. She canned all kinds of vegetables and jellies, and I think she must have had every pickle and cake recipe anyone ever dreamed of! . . . I still treasure her old, mostly handwritten, recipe book and have scanned and categorized these recipes for use by our children and grandchildren.

We had a two-car garage out back, but Daddy had enclosed and floored one side to make a storeroom. Along one side he had built shelves and insulated them so they could be closed off for the winter, holding dozens of jars of all the canned goods Mom was making. Another section held stacks of wood that had been cut in exact lengths to fit the wood-stove. The first chore I remember was to stack these neatly in rows as high as I could reach. A man with a circular saw mounted on the bed of his truck had previously cut these up from all the long left-over slabs that had been bought from the local lumber yard and left in a great pile in the backyard. Every day after school, I had to work at getting these "out of the weather", as well as making sure the kitchen wood-box was filled.

As I got older, I was expected to help mow the yard and weed the garden. I am an only child and was basically a "good boy", but here is where I got into trouble! In my mind, it was either "too hot" or "too cold" outside, or the grass was "too wet."

Dad was a patient man, but he had his limits, so, the sting of his belt on my legs a few times usually resulted in my mowing grass or chopping weeds! It seemed that suddenly it was comfortable outside, or the grass had dried out quickly!

There came a time when he told me, "If you want, you can have this part of the garden for yourself, and you can sell whatever you grow." So, I didn't complain anymore, and, instead of getting a paper route like so many boys my age did, I set up my own "vegetable route". I mounted two large metal baskets on my bicycle and covered several blocks of our community, selling fresh vegetables to the neighbors. They came to expect me on certain days, and I was happy with my own spending money!

In those days, we boys were able to walk right into the "city dump" where the garbage trucks unloaded regularly. There were so many exciting "finds", such as all sorts of army surplus items, and discards from the Fli-back Company that made paddleball sets and other toys. We never knew what we might discover!

Summer vacations usually included at least a two-week stay at my grandfather's farm in Surry County. I was too young to do any real work while I was there, but I have many happy memories of those days. The first car I remember was Daddy's 1931 A-model Ford. He would take us there on the weekend and then leave Mom and me on Sunday evening to return to work on Monday. This car had a metal dashboard, and I always stood between my mother's knees when we traveled. I remember counting the three curves in the road before seeing the old home-place come into view, all the while holding on to the dash with my sweaty hands. I had done this so many times that when Daddy decided to trade in the car, my handprints had been etched into the metal!

While at the farm where Grandpa grew tobacco, I rode the empty sled from the barn back out into the fields were it would be loaded up again with tobacco leaves. These had to be tied in bunches onto long sticks and hung up in the barn to be "cured" by the heat generated from wood burning down below. I tried to stay awake some nights with Grandpa outside the barn where he had to keep putting wood on the fire all night long. I never could stay awake all night, but he had more motivation than I did. After all, this tobacco was his livelihood and its quality when taken to auction would determine how much money he would have to support his family until the next year.

Two of my female cousins spent most of their summers there, and we picked blackberries and got fresh watermelons right out of the field. I was too young for it to make much difference to me, but we had "corn shuckin's", where all the neighbors came on a Saturday night and helped pull the shucks off the big pile of dried corn and put the naked ears into the corn crib. This was accompanied by a great deal of fiddle and banjo playing, and the chance of finding an ear of corn with red kernels, which gave you the right to kiss the person of your choice!

There was lots of this kind of entertainment in those days, without television, cell phones, iPods, and video games! We made our own toys as there were no Wal-Marts around the corner. A family might be blessed with *one* radio, where we could hear the delayed broadcasts of how World War II was progressing in Europe, and maybe a wind-up Victrola that scratched out the sounds from early 78 RPM recordings. Even so, we were happy without all the expensive electronic gadgets being sold today.

My Childhood Home

Favorite Childhood Picture

EARLY SCHOOL DAYS

Things were different in the Forties . . . I walked about a half mile to elementary school every day, usually with my banana and peanut butter sandwich in a "paper poke". Nowadays mothers drive their children to school or meet them at the bus stop, even if it's only a block from their house! I don't remember eating in a school cafeteria until I got to junior high. Since the high schools were further away, I then rode a school bus that stopped about three blocks from our house, in front of Newton's little corner store . . . where cheese and bologna were sold by the slice and candy could be bought for a penny!

I was chosen to be a "school crossing guard" since this was a busy street, and no one dreamed that this would one day be a paid position for adults. Since the junior and senior high schools were side by side, I rode this same bus until 10th grade, when I got my first "wheels".

I'm thankful that we had morning devotionals over the PA system and recited the Pledge of Allegiance to start each day. And, would you believe it, they even taught the Bible as part of the curriculum in high school! Today, we have exchanged the teaching of values and ethics through Bible study and prayer in our schools for metal detectors and policemen (resource officers, if you will). Yet, in those days, students were labeled troublemakers for chewing gum, shooting "spit-wads, or being a bully on the playground. We never heard of bringing knives or guns to school; much less murder on the school-grounds!

God help us to see from whence we've come!

First Grade

School Patrol

Newton's Corner Grocery Store

WHEN "GOD" BECAME MORE THAN A WORD

I grew up in a Christian home, and was taken regularly to church by my parents, who were active members at Hilliard Memorial Baptist located in suburban High Point. As I became old enough, I naturally joined the Boy Scout troop that met each week in the basement of the church.

When I developed an interest in the opposite sex, I either dated girls I already knew in the church, or eventually took almost every date to church with me. In addition to my parents, some of the leaders in the church had a strong influence on my teenage years, which I will detail later. But at this point, I want to share with you how "God" became more than just a word to me.

Of course I had been in Sunday School and Training Union, two worship services on Sundays, and prayer meetings on Wednesday nights all through my adolescent years. Since my dad worked on second shift from 3:00 to 11:00 each night, I often went with Mom to cottage prayer meetings that were held once a month. One of these that still sticks in my mind was in the home of Mrs. Grant, mother of two boys who later became well known in Baptist circles . . . Marse Grant became president of the Baptist Children's Home in Thomasville, and later, Editor of the Biblical Recorder, the state Baptist newspaper. His brother, Worth Grant, became a missionary to Japan after the war. So, I lived in an environment where people didn't just talk about God and Christianity, they *lived it* in front of me.

But it was about 1946, when Billy Graham had just begun evangelistic crusades . . . they were being recorded on the old-style movie reels and shown in other areas of the United States. One of his associates came to High Point to show one of his first films. I can't remember if it was "Mr. Texas" or "Oiltown, USA". A large tent had been set up on a vacant lot downtown, sawdust was covering the ground, and scores of rented chairs were in place for the meeting. Churches of all denominations had announced the presentation, and naturally, I was there with my parents.

I was about ten years old at the time, and all I remember about that night happened at the conclusion of the film. The evangelist announced an invitation hymn, and said, "I want each of you who know beyond any doubt, that if you died tonight you would go to heaven, to please stand." And then it hit me! I couldn't stand! This was the beginning of what I now know was conviction by the Holy Spirit. It became clear to me that, although I had been a "good boy" and never gave my parents or teachers any problems, there was something missing in my life.

For the next two years, at every worship service which ended in an invitation hymn, I felt the same way. Yet, I held on to the pew or squeezed the hymn book a little tighter and stayed in the pew. It was in September of 1948 and I was sitting on the end of the very back pew at our church. I mentioned earlier that I was a part of the Boy Scout troop and this was the regular night for our weekly meeting. However, our church was holding a weeklong revival meeting upstairs, so we came in our Boy Scout uniforms, had a brief meeting, and went as a group upstairs to attend the service. At the time of the invitation, we had sung all the verses of the hymn. Then the pastor said, "I just feel we need to sing another", so he announced a second hymn . . . I never knew if this was on purpose or one of God's "coincidences", but our scoutmaster George Underwood was seated beside me. I knew Mr. Underwood was a committed Christian who taught a men's Sunday school class on Sundays and never kept us out on a camping trip over a Sunday without teaching the Sunday school lesson for the day. As we began to sing the second hymn, he placed his hand on my shoulder and said, "Wouldn't you like to go?"

God used his touch and that question to get me to turn loose of all my hesitation and step out into the aisle. I don't remember walking down the aisle, but I do remember my aunt Ruth sitting beside me on the front pew while I cried tears of joy because of the burden that had been lifted from my spirit. I've never doubted that at the age of twelve, I became a Christian as I asked Jesus Christ to come into my life that night. I've been led to make many other spiritual decisions in my life, but that most important one was settled that night in 1948.

Many years later, I had the honor and privilege to join with another member of that scout troop, who had become a minister, in conducting the funeral service for Mr. Underwood, who had influenced so many lives . . . It was then that I shared these details with his family and I look forward to thanking Him personally in heaven someday!

HIGH SCHOOL AND BEYOND

I've always had a love for reading, which I attribute to my first grade teacher, Mrs. Lee, who had contests based on how many books we read that year. By the time I was in second grade, Mrs. Ballow often asked me to read aloud to the class a story from one of the *Uncle Wiggly* series written by Howard R. Garis in the early Forties. This love of books has served me well, not only through my years of public education, but throughout my life.

High School was easy for me. I had little interest in sports, but instead, occupied myself with indoor activities such as reading, stamp collecting, and home study related to electronics, including radio and TV repair. In fact, with the aid of instructions and parts from a HeathKit, I built our first 17-inch black and white television set as well as several pieces of electronic test equipment. This allowed me to make some money doing radio repairs in a small shop I had set up. Those were the days when radios used vacuum tubes instead of transistors, but by the time color televisions came along, I was into other pursuits.

During my high school years, I was blessed to become a member of the National Honor Society, the Beta Club, the Masque and Gavel Society, and part of the Radio Club that operated an educational FM radio station located at the school. I was asked to serve as general manager of the station in my senior year. The students voted each week for their favorite songs that were being heard on commercial radio and played on their phonographs at home. These votes were counted on Friday mornings and the "Top Ten" were chosen to air on the high school station on Friday afternoons.

This program was picked up by a local commercial station and rebroadcast live to a much wider audience throughout Piedmont North Carolina. I had to make weekly trips to their downtown studio in order to borrow records from their library for use on our program at the school. This connection led to a paid position at their station when I graduated from high school . . . but I'm getting ahead of myself!

High Point High School in the Fifties

My Senior Year

CARS AND JOBS

My first car was a 1939 Ford four-door sedan. A previous owner had installed custom seat covers and it was in great shape inside. I added a set of white-wall tires and gave it a new paint job on the outside. This was a "do-it-yourself project" . . . I took an attachment that included a pint "Mason fruit" jar filled with black paint and attached it to the exhaust of my mother's vacuum cleaner! I taped all the windows and chrome, and did a fairly decent spray job. It really shined, although I know now I could've had a smoother finish if I'd taken the time and used some "elbow grease" to apply rubbing compound before giving it a coat of wax several days later. I've always regretted trading it in on a 1950 Ford some years later!

As soon as I was old enough to look for a summer job, I had my dad take me downtown where I walked and knocked on doors of several businesses, resulting in my first job at High Point Paper Box Company. I worked that summer as a "box stacker". This involved boxes designed to hold a dozen pair of men's socks which were being continuously dropped from a machine onto a conveyer belt. My job was to stack these end-to-end inside each other until there were ten together; turn the stack on it's side and stack another ten; repeating this process until I could lift a hundred boxes at once off onto the floor. This went on all day, and although I was glad to get the 75 cents an hour, I was glad when school started in the fall so I wouldn't have to look at another box!

During my junior and senior years I had accumulated enough credits that I only needed to attend school until one or two o'clock in the afternoon, so I worked in two different hosiery mills in the afternoons. One year I was a "turner", being paid based on how many dozen men's socks I could pull down on a stationary tube like that on a vacuum cleaner and let the suction turn the sock right side out. The other year I was a "knitter", looking after fifteen machines that were making men's socks. This meant I had to keep the different color yarns replenished and cut the socks apart as they came out of the machine as a continuous tube of fabric. Although I only worked four hours and still had time to go out on dates in the evening, I was not excited about making a career of working in the hosiery industry . . . second only to furniture in that area and where most of my whole family had worked all their lives.

So, when I was offered a position at WHPE Radio after graduation, I studied to qualify for a First-class Radio-telephone license and became a transmitter engineer. The transmitters were housed at the base of the broadcast tower which was located five miles out of town in the middle of a large open field away from any other structures. My work there evolved until I also had some "split-shifts", working part of the time downtown as a news announcer, disc jockey, and record librarian. This was a fascinating work for a single person, although I soon found it didn't pay enough to support a family . . . but I'll reserve that for later.

My Disc Jockey Days

LOVE AT FIRST SIGHT

December19,1954 . . . The morning worship service was over and I was about to get in my car, which was parked near the front of the church. As I opened the car door, I looked back one more time and saw Alton Slay coming down the steps with a girl I had never seen before. I just assumed he had brought a date to church. I thought about this all the way home and while we were eating lunch, I said to my parents, "I saw the girl today that I'm going to marry!" Of course, they didn't take me seriously and just thought it was a passing fancy.

However, soon after we had finished our meal, the phone rang. A Christmas drama was being presented that night and both Alton and I were part of the cast. There was to be a dress rehearsal that afternoon, so this was Alton on the phone, asking for a ride to the church. I had to pass right by his house to get there anyway, so this was no problem. This gave me a chance to ask about this new girl, and he said she was not a new date, but was his *cousin,* Louise Parker! She had come to spend the weekend with her favorite aunt and naturally had attended church with them. I was so excited that they told me later that my '39 Ford pulled in their driveway before he could hang up the phone!

After we were introduced, I asked Louise to go with us to the rehearsal. She refused, but I got a second chance. Alton was supposed to bring the wrapped presents to be used by the three wise men coming to see Jesus, but he forgot! So, we returned to his house, and I convinced her to go back to the church with us. She also came to the drama that night, and this resulted in our spending a lot of time together over the next few weeks. I really meant what I had told my parents, so, on January 15, 1955—barely 6 weeks after we had met, she accepted an engagement ring and we began to plan a wedding!

The date had to be changed once, because our pastor had resigned and had accepted a church in Lancaster South Carolina. Since he had counseled with us, and we wanted him to perform the ceremony, we traveled to Lancaster and were married in his home on June 4, 1955. Only our parents were present, along with his family, to witness this special event.

After having to replace a "busted" water hose on the car somewhere near Spartanburg, we celebrated our honeymoon in Asheville and Cherokee, North Carolina. After I signed *Mr. and Mrs. Larry Sledge* for the first time on the registration slip, the motel owner taped it in the front of a paperback book, *The Greatest Story Ever Told*, and gave it to us as a keepsake. She said this was a regular practice for all honeymooners who stayed at her motel! To me, this was just another way God showed us that he was blessing our marriage.

We celebrated our 25th anniversary in Charleston, South Carolina, while serving on the staff of Citadel Square Baptist Church. The theme for that occasion was taken from a song made popular by the Carpenters, "*We've Only Just Begun*". This music was playing in the background then, as well as at our 50th anniversary celebration in Cayce, South Carolina, at Trinity Baptist Church. This is still our favorite song, as we know God put us together at such a young age, and has kept us "young" together ever since! We have just celebrated our 56th anniversary and we feel this song will still be appropriate when we get to heaven . . . We will only have just begun!

In February of 2011, the two of us were honored by being asked to conduct the memorial service for Nellie Slay Beddington, who I credit for being used of God to bring Louise and I together. She was 105 years old, and had outlived her brother and two sisters, two husbands, and most of her friends of that generation. It was during this time that I asked Louise if she had ever stayed a weekend at Aunt Nellie's house before that day in 1954. She said, "No, never before . . . or after!" That caused me to wonder, what would have happened if I had been absent on that Sunday . . . or had simply been looking the other way?

Love at First Sight!
Louise Parker

Our Wedding Day!

BUILDING A HOME

Our first home together was "three rooms and a path", located across the street from my parents on Fala Street in High Point. They had bought the house earlier to be used as rental property and it just happened at the time of our marriage that the tenants had moved elsewhere and it was empty. As a result, Dad offered to let us live there if we would just make his mortgage payment each month instead of paying rent.

I had used the money I had saved to buy wedding rings and a bedroom set, so we found a local furniture store that would sell us living room furniture and a table and chairs for the kitchen with a 90-day same as cash payment plan. They even threw in two end tables, a coffee table and large wall picture at no extra cost! The house already had an electric range but we needed a refrigerator. We signed up for a frozen food plan that included a small refrigerator, and they kept it stocked for about eighteen months with cost of the refrigerator included with the monthly deliveries of food. Some of Louise's friends gave her a "shower" of kitchen utensils and supplies and she did a wonderful job of decorating our new home.

We soon found out that my income from work at a radio station barely covered our expenses and certainly wouldn't provide for a child, if and when God chose to bless us with one. Although we didn't know it would be five years before a "little one" would arrive, I started looking for a better paying job. I well remember one of those early days when money ran out before payday, and I gathered up all the returnable glass coke bottles and took them back to the store. In those days we got two cents per bottle and I collected enough to buy two cans of tomato soup . . . To this day, I still love tomato soup and a grilled cheese sandwich!

After interviews at several companies, I was hired by a dictating machine company with headquarters in Atlanta and trained to be a technician in their Winston-Salem, NC office. The next few years involved plane flights to Atlanta and later, to Hartford, CT, as new products were introduced. I commuted to Winston-Salem each day, until a decision was made to consolidate that office with the one in Greensboro, NC. At that time, we decided to move closer to my work, so we found a house to rent that had indoor plumbing for a change! I was then servicing equipment in hospitals, doctors' and lawyers' offices, as well as various banking and government offices in a ten-county area, so it was good to save on commuting expenses.

Our First Home Together

TWO BECOME THREE

Louise began working for a ladies' clothing store and I began to get involved in sales as well as service at my company, which brought in some extra money in commissions. We soon had enough saved to make a down payment on a house near the church we were attending. We paid $12,900 for a small ranch style house with a mortgage payment of $95.00 a month . . . That would hardly buy a garage today, but for us, it was a major financial decision!

Guess what! Now, after five years, God chose to bless us with our first child . . . Brian Dale was born in August of 1959! God's timing is always right, for about that time I had moved into full-time sales and was later made manager of the Greensboro office, resulting in considerably more income. We found a new church home at Bessemer Baptist and began to get involved there. We had no way of knowing that someday we would be privileged to return to that same church as a member of their staff!

Although they were somewhat older than we were, we became close friends with church members Carl and Louise Kellam, and have many fond memories of vacation trips we made together. He is with the Lord in heaven today, but I smile every time I think about one of our trips to Florida. We were looking for a place to eat, and we walked past a restaurant and looked in the window. Carl said, "No, we can't eat there; they have 'pup tents' on the table!" It was his opinion that if a restaurant had the napkins folded to look like little tents, then the food would be too expensive for us!

After a couple of years, we decided to trade up to a larger house, which resulted in our moving to the other side of the city, not far from where we had first lived in a rented house when we first moved to Greensboro.

Our son, Brian Dale Sledge

CLOTHESLINE QUARTERLIES

My first recollection of really seeing youth work as a *ministry* was sometime in the late Fifties when Louise and I became sponsors of an Intermediate Training Union group. We had both been active in our own churches during our teenage years and had held places of leadership with Beginners and Juniors in the Hilliard Memorial Baptist Church of High Point, North Carolina. However, we never really had a vision of youth *ministry* until my employer transferred us to Greensboro and we became a part of the Florida Street Baptist Church family. We are certain God led us there as we had visited several other churches in the southern part of the city and had deliberately "skipped over" Florida Street because we thought it was too *large.*

Both of us had been accustomed to small churches in High Point and were afraid of just being "lost in the crowd" in such a large congregation as evidenced by the church building at Florida Street. But our plans changed one Sunday afternoon as two ladies came by our home while taking a community census. They were overjoyed to find that we were new Baptist residents in the area. We were so impressed with their warm and outgoing personalities that we surprised them by visiting their worship service that very evening!

We knew at once that God had a purpose for us as part of their church family and moved our membership shortly thereafter. The Lord gave us some blessed experiences over the years as we labored together, but one of the first was in connection with thirteen-year olds in Training Union.

While serving as sponsors of this group, we had many discipline problems—particularly with one boy who was always getting into mischief. He often had to be reminded not to bang the back of his chair against the wall, and on at least one occasion, the class roll book just "accidentally" fell out the second floor window!

But I also recall some serious moments during this time. One of our requirements was that all "quarterlies", as our study guides were called in those days, were hung up on a clothesline strung across the room before we started the program period. The idea was to study your assigned part of the program and be able to share it with the class without reading it from the book. These young people really studied during the week and came prepared on Sunday nights!

What a joy to reflect upon the names of those in that group . . . Charles, Gail, David, Ronnie, "Skipper", Tony, Charlie, etc. Almost every one of them has entered a church-related vocation or has married someone who entered the ministry! I'm sure there were other positive influences in these young people's lives, but I'm grateful that the Lord used "clothesline quarterlies" to help them grow during the time He allowed our lives to touch.

We have learned a deep truth as we have reflected on this period of our lives: That you seldom see the results of youth ministry until years later, and only eternity will reveal the full extent of one's influence on these young lives.

HAIR CURLERS AND DARK PAJAMAS

Some of the most hilarious as well as the most *moving* spiritual experiences have been shared with youth while on retreats and other week-long conferences. Louise actually got involved before I did in this area of youth work, as she served as a counselor for several groups at Fort Caswell Baptist Assembly. One of our most memorable ones was when one of the boys put a live frog in her bed, which was discovered as she turned down the covers one night. At the time, no one ever thought he would take time to get serious about anything, but later Charles Howell married one of the girls from the same group and went on to pastor several churches in the southeast.

I guess the one most hilarious experience for both of us took place at Ridgecrest Baptist Assembly in 1963. We had gone as counselors with about fifteen youth and were staying in Florida Street's private cottage during Youth Conference Week. The boys and girls had been having a running battle all week with little innocent types of mischief, such as rocks sewed up in the pillow cases, salt on the tooth-brushes, home-made exploding caps on the commode seats, etc.

On one particular night, the boys had really mapped their strategy, and knowing the girls always rolled their hair before retiring at night, they decided to sabotage their hair curlers. So, during the afternoon, while we were busy with various activities on the campus, some of the boys used aerosol shaving cream to fill each individual curler with foam, and put them back in their storage bags one by one. But that's only half the story . . .

The cottage was constructed with two bedrooms and bath on each side and no way to get across except through the kitchen, which extended across the back. Louise and the other woman counselor slept on one side with the girls, and I slept on the other side with the boys. Well, I didn't know what the boys had done, but I knew they were taking an unusually long time settling down in bed that night. It seemed that some of them wanted to come into the front bedroom where three other boys and I were sleeping, and I had already sent them back several times to the other bedroom. Actually, I learned later that they wanted to listen though the wall to the girls in their bedroom and hear their cries when the hair curlers were brought out for use.

Well, the boy's bedrooms were separated only by a hanging curtain across the doorway, and I decided to just get up and stand in the doorway to see who it was who persisted in staying out of bed in that other room. It was an unusually dark night and I was wearing navy blue pajamas so no one knew I was standing there. After a few minutes I heard movements and sensed that someone was walking slowly toward me. Now, Charlie must have weighed close to 200 pounds even as a sixteen-year-old, and he couldn't walk softly no matter how hard he tried! I waited until I could barely make out his figure only inches in front of me and then just barely touched his shoulder and said, "Boo!" . . . He let out a yell and fell to the floor where he continued to say, "Oh, Mr. Sledge! Oh, Mr. Sledge!" for several minutes before he could get enough strength to get back on his feet. Well, by that time all the commotion had brought the women counselors and the girls, who were now listening to the boys, instead of vice versa. Needless to say, the girl's hair curlers were forgotten for the night (they were later cleaned and dried out—with the boys help), and I had no problems getting these boys to stay in bed the rest of that week!

Ridgecrest Baptist Assembly, Ridgecrest, NC

ON THE FORT AND IN THE HEART

Many of our early experiences with Youth retreats occurred at Fort Caswell, location of the state Baptist Assembly for North Carolina. Caswell is just that—a deserted fort, a relic of the War, which was purchased by Baptists and made into a summer training site for thousands of adults and youth alike down through the years. In those days, the facilities left much to be desired . . . run-down buildings, no air conditioning, a concrete pool filled with red muddy water. But the spirit of those who attended made up for any lack of more modern facilities which now grace the campus.

One of the favorite gathering places was atop the fort where a cross had been erected and rustic benches provided for an outdoor Worship Center. I well remember one Sunday morning as we sat there looking out over the Atlantic as I taught a Sunday School lesson, titled, "A New Call to Faithfulness", concluding a weekend based on the scripture found in Colossians 1:27, "*Christ in you, the hope of glory.*"

Just the night before we had gathered on the beach below for a campfire service only to realize that no one had brought matches! Even so, our hearts were "strangely warmed" as we sang together above the pounding of the surf. And what an exhilarating experience to sit on that fort and see the sun rise behind that cross—bringing us a new day, and then the sobering realization that one day the Son was raised upon a cross to bring us new life! Needless to say, "Christ in me" took on new significance for many of us who shared that weekend in the summer of '64.

Our son, Brian Dale, was now five years old when God blessed us with another child. A daughter, Tamela Michelle, came into our lives at the end of that year!

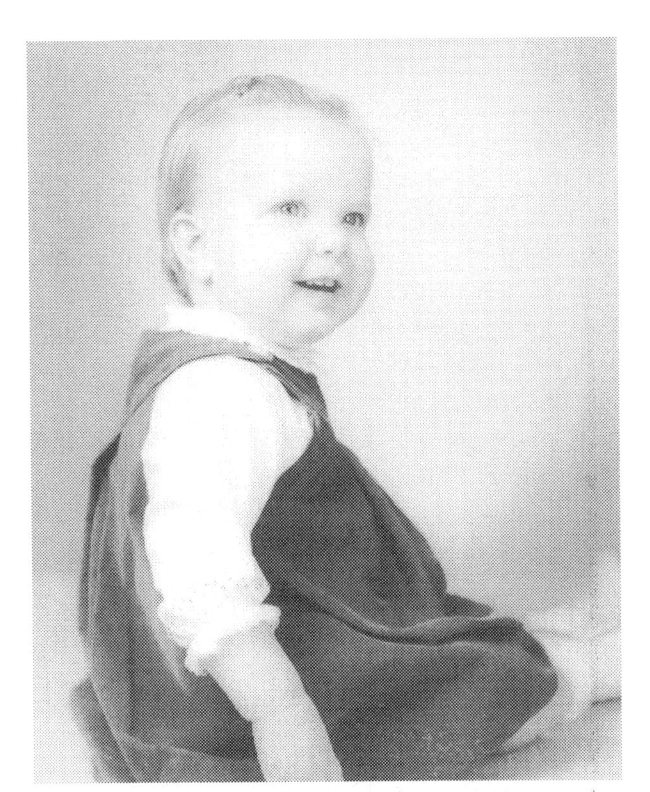

Our daughter, Tamela Michelle Sledge

LOST AND FOUND

The summers of '65 and '66 brought soul-searching experiences of many kinds. I well remember one occasion when our old "white elephant" bus ran out of gas as we were making our way back home. It was a hot day and the sun was beating down on the open country where we had made an unscheduled stop! Our Minister of Music who had been following the bus in his air-conditioned automobile pulled up along-side, and learning of our problem, said, "I'll go on up ahead and find some gas", and quickly drove away. It seemed an eternity before he returned, having driven over 16 miles round trip, to bring us a can of gas. Meanwhile, the restless young people had walked some distance in the opposite direction, seeking shelter of the trees, which could be seen in the distance. They returned and reported, "There's a sign down there . . . It says, 'Shell service station—1 mile'!"

The year before, one of our staff members had lost his eyebrows as he attempted to light the gas oven at our Fort Caswell retreat site!

But both of those experiences pale into insignificance as one young man's name comes to mind. Wayne Poplin, who had been our youth pastor that year, had become active in the youth program only the year before and had begun dating the pastor's daughter, Brenda, during that previous year's youth retreat, also held at Fort Caswell. Wayne had entered Wake Forest University and was pursuing a career in medicine but was having a difficult time making passing grades. We later learned that God was calling him to enter the ministry, but, like so many of us, Wayne was trying to reject the idea of becoming a preacher and was seeking to fulfill his mother's dream of having a doctor in the family. On Saturday night, as the group was gathered around a movie projector viewing a Christian film, Wayne was conspicuous by his absence. Before the film ended, however, be came through the kitchen door, his face white as a sheet, and went straight up the stairs to his room.

He shared the rest of the story the next day. It was well known that he had bought Brenda a bracelet to commemorate their one-year dating anniversary, and that one of the turquoise settings had been lost earlier in the weekend. They had searched for it during the day on Saturday, and that evening he was retracing their steps one more time before returning to the cottage. His path led to the beach and suddenly his inner struggle about school, the call of God, and his future vocation brought him to his knees. As he knelt there in the sand, he became willing to follow God's call into the ministry, but like Gideon, he asked for a sign. He said, "Lord, if that's really what you want me to do, I'll do it . . . but would you confirm it by helping me find that missing stone I've looked for all day?"

He rose from the sand and began the walk back toward the cottage. As he came up the black asphalt street a block or so away, he saw something shining up ahead. As he reached down and picked it up, you guessed it . . . It was a piece of turquoise, lost from a girl's bracelet! Closer examination showed that the tires that had inevitably passed over it during the day had blackened it and it had to be polished to restore its luster!

Wayne *is* a doctor today, having earned his doctorate in theology from New Orleans Baptist Theological Seminary, and with his wife Brenda, is now serving as pastor of a large church outside Charlotte, NC . . . (It was her younger sister, Dianne, who married a medical doctor!)

SAND SPURS AND NEW DIRECTIONS

The year 1967 brought new directions to our lives. I had been employed by a major office equipment distributor for eleven years and was then managing their Greensboro, NC office. I was serving in my church as a deacon, Sunday School Superintendent, and Director of Church Leader Training. My wife, Louise, was equally involved as a Children's Department Superintendent on Sunday mornings and Nursery Coordinator for Sunday evenings. For several months I had grown increasingly more dissatisfied with my job and found myself devoting more time to church-related work. I even searched for other employment, yet felt guilty while doing so. I knew God was calling me to a full-time church-related vocation but was unwilling to give up what I thought was "security" in the business world. My monthly commission checks got smaller and smaller, and by January, 1967, I was tired of the struggle.

It was then that Evangelist Leon Kilbreth came to Florida Street to hold a Sunday School Revival. I somehow anticipated that God would use that week to provide an answer for my uncertain future. The revival services began on Sunday morning and Mr. Kilbreth, who later became our next-door neighbor, spoke to the adults in Sunday School, brought the morning message, and spoke again to a combined Training Union assembly. Then, at the conclusion of his evening message on the Lordship of Christ, he simply stated that there were some folks present who had been holding out on God. He asked that any who felt so impressed might want to come down and kneel at the altar. Twelve people went forward that night and I was in that group!

Finally I was able to give up my so-called "security" and really allow Jesus Christ full control of my life. Two weeks after that experience, a committee from Bessemer Baptist invited me to meet with them regarding their search for a Minister of Education. God is so good . . . He allowed us to begin our ministry there in March, only four miles from our home. At about the same time, our Minister of Music/ Education, Jeff Roberts, had been called as pastor of a church in eastern North Carolina. The folks at Florida Street held a reception to thank him and his wife, "Beanie", for their ministry and to wish them well. Louise and I were asked to serve as host and hostess as the church members came into the fellowship hall. What a great surprise when they presented the Roberts with a going-away gift and then called the two of us to the front. No one had told us that this party was in our honor also! Although I had not been a paid staff member, we were presented with a beautiful silver tray, engraved with our names and the dates of the seven years we had been in their midst. Although we had been Christians for many years, we credit this church and their pastor, Jack Wilder, for helping us really grow spiritually and prepare us for what God was now calling us to do.

There were two humorous events that still come to mind when we reflect on those days . . . We had just bought a home barbering set, and as we were getting ready to go to what we thought was just a reception for our friends, Louise decided my hair needed a trim. So for the first time, she plugged in the barber shears and went to work on one side of my head. Unfortunately, one cut went too deep and I had to try and comb over some hair to cover a spot that stood out like a sore thumb! We went to the reception thinking we could just stay in the background and maybe no one would notice, but just imagine how we felt when we had to come up in front of the whole crowd! A day or so after that experience, Jeff and "Beanie" rang our doorbell and came in with a box of Ritz crackers and a jar of peanut butter. He said, "Churches don't pay much, so you better get used to this; you'll be eating a lot of it in the coming days!" I don't know if this is when it began, but I still keep the pantry stocked with Ritz crackers and peanut butter . . .

God is so good; He gave us eighteen months to adjust to this major change in career as a staff member at Bessemer, before leading us to physically relocate in another city. I well remember our first retreat at Fort Caswell, this time as leaders of the event, rather that just going along as counselors. It seems that this was the time sandspurs were "discovered". We found them in our pillowcases and everywhere we sat down during that weekend! Along with swimming, picnicking, and putt-putt golf, we had spent the first half of the summer meeting weekly in a Backyard Study Course concerning vocational choices. Youth week was held for the first time, built around the theme, "His Way Mine". Jimmy Ward served as our Youth Pastor, and later, with his self-taught guitar music, became the catalyst that developed a real team spirit among the youth. How vivid the memory of his father's question in the parking lot, one week before Youth Sunday, "Do you really think he can do it?" Not only did Jimmy "do it", but he went on to college and seminary and served as a Youth Minister in a South Carolina Church! He later moved to the Columbia, SC area and was a counselor with the Mental Health Department for many years before he and his wife began a medical billing service in Lexington, SC. It was a real treat to recently devote an afternoon to a visit in his home and reminisce about those years at Bessemer Baptist!

ONIONS IN THE POTATO SALAD

Although we served only eighteen months at Bessemer, they were months filled with youth activities. In 1968 the youth group had their first experience at Ridgecrest Baptist Assembly. We had rented a church-owned cottage and fourteen of them became a real "team" as the Holy Spirit moved in all our lives.

There were humorous incidents also throughout the week. The most memorable one was the "potato salad" incident. My wife Louise was in the kitchen preparing one of the many meals of the week. (It seems teen-agers are *always* eating!) As she added the ingredients to make a potato salad, one person came in and said, "I hope you're not putting onions in that . . . I don't like onions!" In a few minutes another came in and said, "You *are* putting onions in that, aren't you? . . . Great!" Then a third one came in and said, "What are you putting in that salad?" Needless to say, no one asked anything about food the rest of that week for I believe Louise made her point that she couldn't cook it fourteen ways!

On one of the lazy afternoons as we gathered on the front porch, someone got the idea that some music would liven things up a bit. (One of our rules for retreats was: no radios, no phonographs, and no tape players!) Two of them finally talked us into going to a Black Mountain hardware store. We came back with a washtub, a 2x4, and some wire. With typical teen-age ingenuity and energy, they soon had a fairly decent "bass fiddle" and the entire group had an enjoyable afternoon songfest!

And what an unexpected delight when Jimmy said, "Our counselors have put up with us all week. They deserve some time to themselves!" . . . It had been a hectic week but we loved every minute of it. Unknown to the young people, we had left Greensboro with a struggle going on inside. A church in Charlotte had contacted us about joining their staff and we had been praying about it for several weeks. I had begun to feel guilty about not having a definite answer for them, especially since the pastor was leaving for a two-week vacation on Monday while we were at Ridgecrest.

Burdened with the desire to know God's will, Louise and I went to the prayer garden during the Training Union hour on Sunday evening. Sitting in our favorite spot overlooking the trickling spring below, we asked God once again to give us some definite sign . . . "Do we go, or do we stay?" About that time one of those frequent afternoon showers sent us scurrying for the auditorium.

Dr. Franklin Paschal was the pastor for the week, and as he spoke from Luke 9:62, his message, "No Looking Back" surely was meant only for us! Then, what joy flooded our souls when one from our group responded to the invitation to trust Christ! He was the only unsaved one of the fourteen, and many of us had been praying that this week would be the turning point in his life. But God wasn't through! The invitation was extended and we were told, "Turn to hymn 425" . . . When our eyes saw the title, "I'll Go Where You Want Me to Go", my hand reached for Louise, and I found her hand already reaching for mine. No word was necessary; we both knew the peace of God's answer!

Well, I was so elated, I wanted to call Charlotte at once, but I also wanted to share Ken's joy in his newfound faith. So we chose instead to return to the cottage, hoping to return to a pay phone later. When I arrived, Ken was already in his room, lying on an upper bunk and just staring at the ceiling. I looked into his face, and he simply said, "I feel so clean inside!" Praise God, what a profound truth from a baby Christian! Isn't God good! Well, shared joy cannot have time limits imposed, and it grew much too late to return to a phone. We went to bed with a resolve to call "first thing tomorrow". Breakfast eaten, I hurriedly returned to the conference grounds and placed the call, only to get a busy signal! Several more times I tried, until, knowing it was too late, I heard the phone ringing. It was 10:30 now, and surely the pastor had left on his two-week camping trip. What a surprise to hear his voice! All I could say was, "What are you doing still at home?" He said, "I don't know . . . I just can't seem to get away!" Finally I could share, "I know the reason . . . you were waiting for my call; you just didn't know it!"

God not only *changes* lives; God also *directs* lives committed to His use.

"CHERISH" IS MORE THAN A WORD

The song by that title still blesses our lives as it floods our memory over the years. Jimmy Ward became quite an accomplished guitar player and, upon our return from Ridgecrest, organized a singing group that was to bless lives in a number of other churches. They dedicated a popular song, "*Cherish*", to us during our final Youth Week at Bessemer. We had made our resignation known by that time, and in September, 1968, we left for Charlotte with an engraved silver tea set and memories worth far more than silver. It was years later when we received a letter from Johnny Bethea, youth pastor during that last Youth Week and now in the military stationed in Oklahoma, that we learned another great lesson . . . We've told many other workers with youth over the years, "It may be years before you see results of your ministry." . . . Johnny had signed his letter, "Your son"! Later, Jimmy Ward led the youth group to record a number of songs and sent them to me on tape. Both the letter and tape are treasured keepsakes from those brief but so meaningful months God allowed us to be a part of those lives at Bessemer Baptist!

As we were getting established in our new work at Midwood Baptist in Charlotte, N. C. we became close friends with the Tadlock family. There was such a wide difference in our ages, yet somehow God just drew us together. We learned that their son, Carlton, had dropped out of college after getting "hooked" on drugs, and had now joined the "hippie" culture. This was a new experience for us, but we felt God leading us to get involved. Little did we know what that would lead to over the next few years!

SPIRITS: HOLY AND OTHERWISE

Our first retreat with the Midwood youth group was to Garden City Chapel near Myrtle Beach in the summer of 1969. We had a great experience as the Holy Spirit worked in many lives and molded the group into a real "family" before our return. We closed one day's activities with a movie entitled "Summer Decision". Many of these youth were facing difficult decisions as the drug culture continued to mushroom in Charlotte and it seemed that "hippies" were everywhere. But on this trip, it seems that some member of a youth group in the adjoining cottage had somehow managed to slip in a fifth of liquor. Two of our boys had joined him in hiding it under a bush at the far end of the vacant lot behind the cottage, planning to slip out of bed that night and share it. It's difficult, if not impossible, to keep secrets in a group of twenty youth, so before nightfall one of our counselors had been told of the plan. After lights out, it seemed the boys dorm became quiet a lot earlier than usual! A short while later two boys tiptoed out the door, with a wide-awake counselor following a few moments behind. Sure enough, he caught the three "conspirators" at their chosen bush with the forbidden bottle in hand!

This event triggered a series of counseling opportunities and the resulting attitudes among the entire group released the Holy Spirit's power in an unusual way! There was little sleep that night, but I can still see little groups of three or four huddled in impromptu prayer circles in the kitchen, on the porch, and behind the bus parked out front. Carlton Tadlock came down for the weekend, and although he remained "on the fringe" of youth activity over the next few years, this episode became one of many that the Holy Spirit used to draw him back to God. Even the undesirable actions of Neal and Eddie were used of God to bring His plan more in focus for a number of youth.

THE "FLYING SHINGLES" INCIDENT

Twelve of the Midwood youth attended their first Youth Conference at Ridgecrest Baptist Conference Center in July 1970. We had rented a private cottage on the side of a mountain some distance away from the main assembly grounds. The secluded location really helped us develop a family atmosphere during our stay but it also was destined to provide the backdrop for a serious, although comical, incident on the weekend. As the story unfolded later, it seems that David and Neal had noticed some torn pieces of roofing shingles around the edge of the sun deck, which was built on top of the house. Arriving back at the house before any one else after morning classes, it seemed the most natural thing in the world to sail these "Frisbee shingles" across the road and down into the valley below. But while they were engaged in their contest to see who could sail theirs the greatest distance, a car came by! . . . Just then, one of the shingles fell short of its goal, hitting the top of the car as it passed below.

A few hours later, a campus security guard was knocking at our door. By that time we had finished our lunch, and Louise and another of our counselors were in the kitchen peeling potatoes for our evening meal! I still wonder what that guard thought when two women opened the door with butcher knives still in their hands!

He relayed to us the complaint that someone had lodged, "someone is throwing rocks at cars from that house." of course, we were unaware of what had happened and could only assure him that we would check it out and take appropriate action. I had begun the week by telling our group at our first nightly devotional time, "While we are here, we are a family. What each of us does this week will affect all the others. If any problem arises we will deal with it on that basis." So when we gathered that evening and after the devotional and a sharing time related to the day's activities, I referred back to those earlier remarks. I then told the group of the visit by the security guard and said, "I know who did it, (one of the fellows had joked about it with one of the girls and she had told a counselor) but I'm not going to embarrass you by calling your names. You will remember my words to you on our first night together . . . that each of our actions is a reflection on the group, and while we are here we are a family. So, I think we should sit here together until you are willing to admit to the group that you did it."

Well, the silence was deafening, but after a few minutes, which seemed an hour, one of the girls got impatient and complained of being sleepy. She said, "They must have made a mistake; nobody threw any rocks from this house!" And two fellows chimed in, "There weren't any rocks thrown from here; let's go to bed." But I felt a lesson could be learned from this experience, so I said, "No, I told you I know who did it, and we'll stay up all night until we settle this." In a few more minutes, one of these same two fellows sheepishly said, "We didn't throw any *rocks*, but we did throw some *shingles*!" David Holloway went on to complete his seminary training and has served as a youth director and as an associate pastor in several churches. He now is senior pastor at a church in Lumberton, NC. There were other memorable incidents during that week. Gay Nunn got lost when she tried a short cut back to the cottage one night, and Lori Patton is the only one we ever knew who fell *up* the stairs! Gay went on to play piano at a mission in Ghana where her husband's company sent them. Lori later married a young man who was already serving as a minister of education and she became choir director in a near-by church.

"Being Christ-like became more than a study theme that week and lives are still being changed as a result!

THIS . . . IS LIFE?

1970 brought many other exciting experiences as the Holy Spirit began to mold a team of youth and caused them to look beyond themselves. They prepared the "LIFE" musical and presented it in twelve different places over a period of months. We still have a tape of one of their concerts among our keepsakes. Seventeen of them held a Youth Revival in Hickory, NC, and The New Life Generation Singers became really concerned about reaching lost people through music. As they reached out to others, their own level of discipleship deepened, and Louise and I were challenged to keep pace with their spiritual growth.

We needed these experiences in our own lives to strengthen us for what lay ahead. In March of 1970, I received a call from Carlton's "hippie" girlfriend just as I was making the transition from Church Training to the evening worship service. She said he was very sick but wouldn't let her call his parents or a doctor. They were in a hotel room downtown and she wondered if I could come down and convince him to see a doctor. I had never been able to get beyond having lunch with Carlton several months earlier as he seemed satisfied with his way of life. We had been praying for him and I saw this phone call as an answer to prayer. I assured the girl that I would be there as soon as I fulfilled my responsibilities in the service, but when I heard the name of the hotel I knew I could not go alone. Carlton's dad was serving as an usher that night and after a brief explanation we were in his car and on our way. The hotel was located in a very undesirable neighborhood and I left Mr. Tadlock in the lobby with instructions, "If I'm not back in fifteen minutes, come up after me." I must say I entered that elevator with some misgivings, yet certain that God was going to use this incident to His glory.

When I found the fifth floor room, I saw that it was crowded—two girls and three young men, and it became clear that they were all living there together. I was unable to persuade Carlton to see a doctor, nor would he agree to let me take him to his parent's home. In the hour since his girl friend had called she had gone out for some soup and persuaded him to eat it. Seeing that I could do nothing more to help one who wanted no further help, I invited the entire group to a concert by the Spurrlows to be held in a few days at a local high school. And then Jerry Hill, better known as "J.C." among his friends, asked "Who are the Spurrlows?" He said he had a sister who had toured with the Young Americans singing group some years before. After leaving my number and asking them to call me if Carlton got worse, I made my way back down to the lobby. It took some persuasion to get Mr. Tadlock to leave without seeing his son, but I assured him that it would only make matters worse if he went upstairs. We were not privileged to see God turn Carlton's life around, but, many years later, we learned that he became employed as a counselor in the drug rehab program in Mecklenburg County. He also became a vestryman in the Episcopal Church and served the Lord for many years before his death from lung cancer a few years ago. However, this hotel visit eventually led to several of the "hippies" attending our church, especially the evening services. Jerry became interested in Carlton's sister, Cheri, who could best be described as "a breath of fresh air" in comparison to Carlton's friends. Jerry may have attended church with wrong motives but that's the only place Cheri would take up any time with him.

On one occasion Louise invited Jerry, Cheri and Carlton to our home for dinner. As it turned out, Carlton didn't want to come without Joy, his girlfriend, and both wanted to bring along another friend, David. Well, we set five extra places at the table and the whole group came. Weeks later, Jerry confessed that he was on LSD at the time, and his steak kept "moving around all over his plate". We learned something that night—"hippies" never went anywhere alone, they always went in groups! Cheri joined in our concern to try to reclaim some of these youth who were wasting their lives on drugs and loose living. Jerry kept trying to get a date, but she just kept telling him she would sit with him at church. Knowing his fear of being caught alone with "straight" people, we were greatly surprised when Cheri called to tell us one day that Jerry wanted to come over alone to talk to us. Our invitation to dinner had so surprised him that he just had to come back and "check us out". It was on this visit that I presented the plan of salvation to him and marked the verses of the "Roman Road" in a New

Testament, which I gave him. He was so much under conviction that he could hardly hold a cigarette with which he was trying to control his nerves. Suddenly he sprang up from the sofa and said, "I've got to go!" I urged him to take the New Testament with him and to read over again the verses I had marked. We learned later that he had gone to some solitary place and sat in his car while reading over those verses and the one I had written on the flyleaf, "I am the Way, the Truth, and the Life . . .". A few days later, during an evening revival service, he almost ran down the aisle in such a dramatic conversion experience that it stirred the entire church.

Over the weeks that followed, he took me to many places (that I would never have gone alone) where he shared his testimony with a number of his friends in the drug culture. He was living with a relative who only used him to steal tape players to support a drinking habit, and we knew that environment was no place for a new Christian. So we "adopted" him into our family and he came to live with us. He was used of God to lead several weekend youth revivals and had opportunities to share his testimony in many locations.

But his old friends continued to pull at him and because of his past, our phone was even tapped for a time. He even moved to another city and tried to make it in a new job, but he finally decided to enlist in the army in an effort to get away from his old way of life. He was soon trained in helicopter maintenance and sent to Vietnam, where all manner of drugs were available on every hand. He shared with us later that twelve-year olds would stand at the entrance to the military installation with drugs for sale! Needless to say, in that lonely environment, he was not yet strong enough to resist. Discharged from the service with a medical discharge, and after several weeks in a San Francisco hospital, he was sent home . . . back to our home which was the only home he had known since he had left at seventeen to live communal style in the ever-changing "hippie" culture. For almost six months he never left the house without one of us, for fear he would run into some of the old crowd. Finally the day came when he felt strong enough to make it on his own so he rented a place across town and moved out once again. Hopefully, he had learned the secret of really *living,* and, although the very foundations of our marriage had been shaken, Louise and I became even more convinced that "Love is something you *do*!"

Jerry Hill with Tamela and Brian

GOD DON'T MAKE NO JUNK!

The conversion of Jerry Hill and the experiences in dealing with so many others who where still in the "hippie" drug culture brought a new level of seriousness to the youth of Midwood Church. Several of them attended the Youth Evangelism Night at the Greensboro Coliseum in February of 1971. Jerry was a part of the group by then and he was so touched by the message by Dr. Leighton Ford that he talked about it for days. When I told him that Dr. Ford lived in Charlotte, he begged me to get an appointment with him. I wasn't too optimistic about it when I made the phone call, but I was pleasantly surprised that Leighton invited us over later that same week. We enjoyed a couple of hours over iced tea that afternoon as Jerry told his life story and asked for advice about entering the ministry. He left with an autographed copy of Dr. Ford's latest book, *One Way to Change the World*, and a resolve to at least visit Gardner-Webb College to investigate the possibility of pursuing college studies. He later abandoned the idea when he learned he would have to get his father's signature on a financial aid form before his application could be processed.

I invited him to share his testimony at an associational outreach meeting which I had been asked to lead in Waxhaw, NC. This opened up several opportunities for him to lead weekend youth revivals in Charlotte and the surrounding area.

In July, thirteen from our youth group attended Youth Conference at Ridgecrest Baptist Assembly. Jerry was unable to go as he had moved to Burlington, NC, where he was opening up a new branch of a drapery cleaning business. The conference theme was *Being Me* and a highlight of the week was the sessions led by Grady Nutt based on his book by the same title. In his vernacular, "God don't make no junk" became the byword for the week. Many of them began to deal with feelings related to self-worth and self-confidence; they really began to see the "masks" we sometimes wear, and a new spirit of openness and love for one another developed. As counselors, we had a beautiful week of simply sharing in what God was doing in the lives of these young people, but one particular incident marked the week with some extra excitement.

We were staying in a two-story house, and Mary Allen fell as she started down the stairs on Saturday night. She was dating Rodney Evans at the time, and he helped us get her to the infirmary. We all feared that her ankle was broken, and the nurse called ahead to an Asheville hospital where we were to get it x-rayed. Rodney's best friend, Don, had come up for the weekend so he wanted to go with us. Now, Don had been known to get his share of "pink slips" from the guardians of our highways, so I knew this would be a night to remember if he drove the car. But Rodney got behind the wheel and Don and I jumped in the front seat. Louise got in back with Mary and the five of us were on our way.

The hospital was about seventeen miles from Ridgecrest, but with Don telling Rodney, "Faster, faster!" we made the trip in eight minutes! We passed three parked patrol cars on the way, and either the patrolmen were asleep, or too busy drinking coffee somewhere to see us fly past! Rodney was a nervous wreck by the time the emergency room crew actually treated Mary, almost a half-hour later. She nursed a bad sprain and walked with a crutch the rest of the week, but she was walking fine some years later when she came down the aisle to meet a smiling Rodney on their wedding day! Theirs was the first marriage ceremony in which I was asked to participate! There have been many others through the years but that first one has a special place in our album of memories.

NEVER SAY, "GOODBYE"

The summer of '72 found us back in the same house at Ridgecrest with an even larger group of young people. This was a week filled with many special experiences as the theme focused on "Being A Disciple". The scripture from Ephesians 3:20-21 took on new meaning in our lives and I believe God allowed us to experience just a little taste of heaven during this particular conference. Rather than try to add details and highlight only the major happenings of the week, I have chosen to use the report that Louise shared with our church as the basis for this chapter. We submit it as evidence that one can have fun *and* be a growing Christian at the same time.

WHAT GOING TO RIDGECREST MEANS:

Living for a week with twenty young people.

Trying to please twenty different appetites at mealtime.

Sleeping downstairs under nine girls . . . who must walk the floor all night long!

Going upstairs to say, "We must stop talking, it's almost time to go to classes."

Being awakened by spoons on pots and pans as your alarm clock.

A midnight trip to an Asheville hospital for x-rays after someone falls down the stairs.

Having to say, "I'm sorry" because someone misunderstood me.

Someone coming down the stairs saying, "Louise, we need you" . . . going upstairs and finding one who has fainted lying in the floor.

Boys chasing a bat around the cottage and killing it with a broom while the girls scream.

Telling them not to bring bugs or animals in the house.

Sending the boys back out with a turtle—"No, you can't put it in the girl's bedroom!"

Getting aspirins for them when they have a headache.

Trying to talk above the roar of the tape player.

Learning that someone else knows how to turn out lamps too!

Trying to decide which makes the best room deodorant-wood smoke or lemon spray.

Hearing someone hit the ground—"No, that can't be one of ours; but it is!" . . . Lori fell UP the stairs after the Lake Dew vesper service!

Finding corn flakes in your pillow.

Losing your pajamas . . . "I'm sure I put them back in that drawer this morning; how did they get inside the piano?"

Looking for your bedroom shoes and finding the toes stuffed with paper.

Asking, "Now, who ate my flashlight?"

Lying in bed and hearing dozens of empty coke cans come rolling down the stairs—accompanied by a shower of confetti coming from the balcony.

All the girls finding pine needles in their beds . . . Then telling them to clean their rooms.

Sending the boy's back because they didn't clean under the beds.

Falling down the mountainside while on a sunrise hike.

Ducking your head under the covers when two empty coke cans come flying mysteriously through the air.

Being told to stay in the kitchen while the young people go up on the sun porch to count pennies and nickels to go buy you a souvenir from the gift shop.

Waking up with someone standing in the doorway yelling, "Be calm! Everything's going to be all right!"

Gathering around the fireplace at 10:00 each night for devotions.

Going to the Prayer Garden and finding two of our group who come over and join us in prayer.

Calling four of them into the living room and praying together after a misunderstanding.

A young lady coming down the stairs after everyone is in bed, saying, "I need to talk with you" . . . . After talking a while, getting on our knees in front of the fireplace and asking God to hear and answer her request.

Someone saying as they go up the stairs, "I'll have devotions tonight if you want me to."

Standing in a circle singing, "There's a Sweet, Sweet Spirit in This Place."

A young man turning and putting his arms around you, saying, "I've just given my whole self to God!"

Hearing someone say to another young person, "I love you because God made you."

Listening to someone pray aloud and in a group for the first time.

Hearing a young man say, "God, there are some things on the inside that need to be removed—will you please remove them?"

Nine or ten young people going together over to the Prayer Garden—praying and reading the Bible, then coming back and sharing what they feel God has said to them.

Someone saying, "Thank you for telling us about the Prayer Garden."

A young man walking up to the Prayer Garden with you and telling you how he feels about what God has for him—then praying about it together.

A group of ten going back to the Prayer Garden—God leading a young man to find scriptures that they need to hear.

Getting a letter from home asking that we pray for a special need—Some of us stopping and praying for this person right then.

Someone saying, "If you hadn't loved me, I never would have gone this far."

A young man saying, "I believe God is leading me into this particular occupation-I'm going to step out on faith and see if this is it."

Standing in Dew Garden at a campfire service singing, "Holy Spirit, Breathe On Me", as a young person moves closer and puts her arm around you . . . feeling God's presence so close as you turn to leave.

Watching the youth during the worship services—seeing them almost on the edge of their seats as the minister has their undivided attention.

Breaking bread together as we "Celebrate Life" in the final worship service—gaining a fresh understanding of Jesus feeding the five thousand—almost as if we were sitting there on the mountainside.

A young lady turning to you and saying, "I've been a Christian for a long time but I haven't been a real witness for Him—if God will help me, I'm going home and share Jesus with my friends."

Sitting around the kitchen table talking about what Christ means to us and how we can show His love both inside and outside our church.

A group of ten down on their knees at 1:00 in the morning praying that the Holy Spirit will be able to work in our church at home.

Standing in your special place in the Prayer Garden with the one who God has given you as a life partner and rededicating yourselves to His will as you are used in His service.

As you pull out of the driveway to return home, hearing someone say, "I'm not going to look back; I'm not going to cry."

An experience with God and His children that will be remembered until we meet Him in heaven some day . . . One of our most prized possessions is the plaque the youth gave us at the end of that week. It's message, "Heaven is where friends will no longer say 'Goodbye' to one another", came to have an even deeper meaning for our family only a month after our return. Read on . . .

THE VERSE THAT GOT HIM IN

Ministering to youth has its humorous moments as we have shared with you thus far, but there are also times when these have been mingled with tears. Such a time came to our family on August 25, 1972, when a phone call shocked us with the news that Jerry Hill had been found dead in his own bed that morning. An autopsy revealed no conclusive evidence and we will probably never know the real cause of his death. But of one thing we are certain, Jerry had earlier met Jesus Christ and even his death bore witness to the fact that only in the Son can be found "the Way, the Truth, and the Life".

The setting for his funeral service was a chapel near Freedom Park in Charlotte. He had been known for years by so many of the "hippies" and drug users who often frequented this park that many of them were actually present for the service. I saw this as a real opportunity to share the gospel with so many who might not have another chance to learn of God's love.

Relying on my favorite scripture verse, "*I can do all things through Christ which strengtheneth me*" (Philippians 4:13), I used the following words as part of the service in an attempt to get them to look inward and really consider their lifestyle before it was too late.

"Each one of us in our more serious moments, must admit that there are basically three things for which we search in this life:

1. A *direction* or *purpose* for our lives
2. Real *truth* in the midst of hypocrisy
3. And something to make *life* really worth living

The answer to our search is summed up in these words of Jesus—"*I am the Way, the Truth, and the Life . . .*" On March 9, 1970, Jerry Hill found the *WAY*—when God reached down deep inside and touched his heart. He found a direction for his life as he began to follow Jesus Christ. Although our hearts are heavy and there's an empty spot because one we love is no longer with us on this earth, we can be comforted by the fact that he is now with Jesus as a result of that experience.

Jerry never stopped in his search for *TRUTH*. His favorite word was, "Why?" He was not satisfied with easy, pat answers in a world of injustice. He had an unusual ability to see what was inside a person regardless of outward appearances.

In his search for truth, he was seeking that which would make *LIFE* worth living, not only for himself, but also for others. Someone has listed four approaches to life:

1. We can run our own lives in our own human strength.
2. We can run away from life by use of the many crutches available today.
3. We can run with the crowd—letting them make our decisions for us.
4. We can present our lives to Jesus Christ—and let Him run our lives for us.

At one time or another, Jerry tried all four, but—lest we think less of him, let us remember that most of us, too, have done the same, at least to some degree. Although it hurts us to give up a loved one, we can be thankful today that God in His great mercy reached down again and called Jerry home. He no longer has to run—he's at peace with Jesus. Jerry felt for many years that God wanted him to preach. Although it was a struggle for him, he fulfilled that calling for a period of time in the spring of 1971. Some of you are here today because God touched you through his life.

But Jerry probably preached his greatest sermon last Friday as he passed from this earthly life to a better life in another place. It's almost like I can hear him saying, "Only one approach to life is the right one . . . learn from my experience—

— Don't try to run your own life—you'll make a big mess!
— Don't run away from life—you can't run far enough to get away from yourself.

— Don't run with the crowd—be the individual God created you to be—
— But let Jesus run your life—He really meant it when he said, *'I am the Way, the Truth, and the Life.'*
— Don't continue to grieve over my leaving—But look around you . . .
— Find someone to love—Love them enough to share Jesus—But remember, you may get hurt in the process . . ."

I found the following words among Jerry's notes and feel compelled to share them:

"Getting hurt is part of loving people. Christ loved us and He hurt so much that His sweat turned to blood and His soul departed from His body. The only gift of love that you can give to Christ when you get to heaven is the love that you have given to others. Everything else already belongs to Christ."

Thank God for His gift of love to Jerry Hill . . . and to each of us.

"JOY . . . OR HAPPINESS?"

1973 was a year of deepening spiritual growth among the youth of Midwood. The death of Jerry Hill caused many of them to get serious about following Jesus Christ. The church owned a small house on an adjoining lot that had been rented out in the past. The youth group had outgrown their meeting rooms so the church decided to use it for all the youth activities and free up some space for other age groups in the main building. At about the same time, a long-time Sunday School Superintendent who was well respected by the young people died that year. As evidence of how much trust the adults had come to have in the youth, they agreed to name the building the "Bill Queen Youth Center" and permitted us to give a key with an engraved key tag to each young person. They were instructed that they were only to use it on Friday nights when we planned to open it for fellowships after football games . . . We contacted Duke Power Company and were able to get about a dozen of the large empty cable spools to use as tables in the building. These were then covered in colored tablecloths to give it a "coffee-house" atmosphere. Louise and Shirley Stroud were the Youth Sunday School leaders at that time, and the youth were so excited to have their own "space" for both morning and evening every Sunday!

Summer found us at Ridgecrest again with a group of nineteen of them engaged in a week of activities based on the theme, "Being Joyous". Development of this theme throughout the week impressed upon us a major truth . . . *Happiness* depends on outward circumstances; but real *joy* comes from within, even in the midst of this pressure-cooker world in which we live. We stayed in a new location this time, sharing a large house nestled in the trees some distance away from the main conference activities. Our group developed a greater "retreat spirit" as they shared more actual time together, and this house became an annual "home away from home" for several summers to follow.

The prayer garden had been largely overlooked by the youth in previous years as they had been there primarily as a group and only at a counselor's insistence. But this summer found many of them returning to the cottage in groups of three or four, telling us of their experiences in the prayer garden! Of course, we all still went there as a group, and in those quiet moments many of them openly shared what Christ was doing in their lives. Kim Wyatt gave his testimony of his relationship with Jesus Christ as he used the nearby moss and twigs to symbolize three crosses on a hillside, saying, "That's what Christ did for me!"

"Tinker" Outlaw (yes that's his real name!), who later married Kim's sister, Nina, came to really know Jesus Christ as Savior and Lord during this week. "Tinker" became one of a nucleus of five youth who joined me in starting a teen-age "Serendipity Club" at nearby Fountain Square Apartments. But that's another story, reserved for another chapter . . .

Not everything that happens that make such a retreat memorable are of such spiritual significance . . . Leaders of the conference center repeatedly warned that the train tunnel was "off limits" to everyone. The railroad ran between the conference grounds and many of the church-owned cottages that housed groups such as ours. A tunnel had been constructed years earlier to allow the railroad to go under the highway and on up into the mountains. It seems that whatever is forbidden is always more attractive to teen-agers, and ours were no exception! Our own son, Brian, along with Debbie Walker and Frieda Loftis, decided they had to see this tunnel close-up. Then Debbie decided she just had to walk through it! Fortunately no train was nearby at the time, but, as you might imagine, they had some public "confession time" when we found out about it . . . Debbie went on to become Activities leader for Seniors in a large Charlotte church, and Frieda became WMU director in her church!

We were doubly blessed that summer as we planned a "Youth-quake" for the Midwood community, which was led by Don Moody, one of the young men from Florida Street Baptist in Greensboro. He had followed God's leading into the preaching ministry several years earlier, and had now finished seminary and been called as pastor of a church on the outskirts of Greensboro. His youthful enthusiasm spurred the Midwood Youth to even greater emphasis on personal discipleship. Later that same year we had twenty youth involved in a Thanksgiving retreat at Ridgecrest. The emphasis of the weekend was "Prayer: the

Language of the Spirit." Their "Letters to God" and home-made color slides depicting their relationships to God were only two of many creative activities that drew us closer to Him and to each other. Our times together became more and more of what I consider a foretaste of heaven and an illustration of the scripture, "*Behold, how they love one another . . .*"

FORMAL BEACH ATTIRE?

During these exciting years at Midwood, we not only had many memorable times with teen-agers, we also enjoyed some humorous moments with some of their parents!

On one occasion, we found ourselves on vacation at Myrtle Beach with Gene and Ann Wyatt where we had booked adjoining rooms at a beach-front motel. Gene was always kidding me about never seeing me without a necktie, so I decided to make a joke out of it . . . We were getting dressed to go down to the beach, and when we emerged from our rooms, I was wearing swim trunks and a bright yellow tie around my neck! I thought we would have to pick Gene up off the floor as he doubled over in laughter . . . I had just asked, "Am I not properly dressed?"

We also vacationed many times with Jim and Shirley Stroud, who owned a timeshare in North Carolina and often exchanged their week for other locations in the United States. We traveled with them to New York City, the Pennsylvania Amish Country, and other lesser known areas of the East Coast. However, the two most memorable times took place during a week at Sugar Mountain in North Carolina. Although we have now been gone from Midwood Baptist for over 35 years, we still meet for lunch every few months, and often re-live these two events . . .

On the day before, without telling Jim or me, Louise and Shirley had held aside four very large strawberries and placed them in the refrigerator. The others we had bought were consumed that same day, so these were being reserved to top off a special dessert the next evening. Well, as soon as we arrived at the condo, Jim had staked his claim to the very center of an L-shaped sectional sofa, so when the other three of us decided to go out shopping, he chose to stay in and take a nap. Sometime during the afternoon, he obviously woke up wanting a snack, so he opened the refrigerator to view some choices. These juicy strawberries were too much of a temptation, so he enjoyed one of them along with whatever else he could find. You should have heard Shirley later as she discovered one missing, "What happened to that strawberry? . . . There were four of them and now there are only three!" It didn't take long to find the guilty party as Jim sheepishly replied, "I ate it!" You can then imagine how we really made a big production out of eating the remaining ones that evening, while he only had a *memory* of how delicious they were!

This was also the trip where our wives decided the upstairs Jacuzzi would be a good place to add some bubble bath . . . They just didn't count on how efficient it was, and they overdid it when they poured in the liquid. In a few minutes, we heard them call downstairs for help! When Jim and I raced up the stairs, we saw the two of them standing in the tub in their bathing suits and using a plastic wastebasket to try and skim away some of the bubbles that were already more than waste deep! After we fell over laughing at the top of the stairs, Jim ran back down to get his video camera. He recorded this "funniest home video" that was shared with some other family members when we returned home, and we relived that experience for months to come!

LET'S GO TO THE HOP

In April of 1974, our church held a "Festival of Faith". I've never been involved in anything like it before or since! It started out to be a lay renewal weekend but became far more than that. As we planned the activities, we felt a need to expose our church family to Christians from other denominations. Many factors had resulted in a church that had become ingrown and as the years went by, the adults became more resistant to change. So we started out by asking "Bud" Carrier, vice president of a local bank and an active Presbyterian, to coordinate the weekend. "Bud" had led several lay renewal activities, and he and his wife were involved in a follow-up weekly support group. He enlisted about a dozen spirit-filled Christians from three states to come and help us. There were Baptists, Methodists, Presbyterians, Lutherans, and one Catholic in the group. But we soon lost sight of denominational labels as they opened their lives to us, and we saw each other as brothers and sisters in Christ. During the weekend this team led several sharing times in selected homes and gave testimonies at a men's luncheon and a ladies coffee hour. "Bud" himself led two morning Bible studies for all the team and our church staff. His exciting presentation, "Possessing the Promised Land" brought the Old Testament to life and opened up a whole new approach to Bible study I had never seen before.

But that was only the beginning . . . We also invited Ross Rhoads, pastor of a local independent Presbyterian church, to preach for us during two revival-type services and asked Jerry Thomas, owner of a local music store and part-time music minister in a Methodist church, to hold a sacred concert on Saturday night. Jerry's presentation of Bill Gaither's "Alleluia, A Praise Gathering of Believers" was a never-to-be forgotten experience. It was also during this time that we met the "Peace Trio", which later came to mean much to our lives. David Holloway, who you met in an earlier chapter (remember the flying shingles?), had joined with two girls from a nearby Presbyterian church to form this group. Some of their original compositions were later used of God to speak to us as we faced another transition period in our walk with Him. But that's getting ahead of myself . . . The "Festival of Faith" may not have had as great an impact on anyone else, but "Jesus Christ is Lord" took on fresh meaning to me.

None of us has walked far in our spiritual journey until we learned that the devil doesn't like radiant, spirit-filled Christians who are excited about sharing their faith. As we get outside ourselves and the four walls of our churches, we begin to infringe on his territory, and he retaliates! One of his favorite tactics is to bring division and cause discouragement. Within weeks after the "Festival of Faith" we began to notice a division among our youth group. As we made our way for the fifth year in a row to Ridgecrest, there was dissension developing for no apparent reason. We especially wanted this week to be a good experience, as for the first time, we had taken along four parents to help with transportation and cooking. Cecelia Hattrich made history as she looked at the pile of groceries and exclaimed, "Who's going to eat all this?" As veteran youth counselors, we weren't worried about *that* problem!

Over 1200 youth were involved that week in study and activities built on the theme, "Being Creative". Louise not only served as a counselor for our group . . . she also bought the food, supervised the cooking, served up eighteen delicious meals on time, and provided between-meal snacks . . . all at a cost of only $1.80 per person per day. That's what I call, "being creative"!

David Holloway was now serving as a summer youth worker in Darlington, South Carolina, and nine of the young people from his church joined our "family" that week. After overcoming some initial differences in the group, it turned out to be one of our best weeks together. Two of the many events of that week were especially meaningful to me. My memory reflects on that afternoon in the living room when an impromptu songfest turned to the songs of the Fifties. To really get in the act, several of the youth went to their rooms to dress the part. A few minutes later the girls returned with bobby sox, pigtails, and extra make-up. The boys had greased down their hair and combed it back in "duck-tail" fashion and they all began singing "Let's Go To The Hop", a song made popular by Chuck Berry during the Fifties era. Louise and I had a great time watching them and reminiscing about our dating days! But the real reason this experience meant so much to us was that Patricia Haga was now a part of the group! She had grown up in the church and since becoming a part of the youth group had been considered just a "wallflower". She was very timid, seldom spoke, and wore little or no make-up. But to see her now! Frieda and Joyce had loaned her some clothes, helped her with a new hairstyle and make-up . . . and presto! She had blossomed into a whole new personality.

The scene on my memory screen shifts to another day, and another place. Several of us are now seated in the Prayer Garden at Johnson Spring. Somehow, in God's providence, He had brought me to that sacred place as the only adult in the group. As we meditated and prayed together, Frieda Loftis slipped up closer to my side and shared something she had never told anyone, "God has called me to be a missionary". As the impact of that statement took a few minutes to really sink in, she confessed, "I'm afraid". No amount of money could buy that experience from me! Thank God that in His own timetable He had permitted me to share these precious moments with one of His children.

Frieda later married David Norris, a fine young man who had recently become more involved in our youth group. She went on to college and seminary—completing nurse's training as well as studies in Religious Education. For the present, God has chosen to leave her and David in their hometown of Charlotte where she is a "missionary" to college students. The last time I saw her she was Director of the College Department in her church and serving on the nursing staff of a local hospital. She later became Director of the Woman's Missionary Union in her church where she continued to involve others in missions. At the time of this writing, she and David now have three college-age children, and the whole family has been on several short-term mission trips . . . Who knows what God still has in store for their future!

There were many other important decisions made that week. Debbie Walker opened herself to God's will—"Maybe God doesn't want me to become a 'Sunday's child'"; our son, Brian, was strengthened in his faith, and one of the Darlington girls, Libby, led a young boy to Christ. That's especially significant, since she had only been a Christian for eight days!

Our report service to the church upon our return was really a Worship Celebration that could best be summed up by the theme song we used, "I feel good, good, good; every time I think about Jesus, I feel good . . ." Only a month later many of these same youth attended the State Youth Evangelism Night in Greensboro Coliseum. Evangelist Richard Hogue challenged the thousands of young lives there assembled to "stop playing games" and get busy for Christ. I continue to thank God for the good reports we hear from so many of those youth, and for letting us just be a small part of those exciting days of decision.

Midwood Baptist Youth Group

SERENDIPITY AND SORROW

1974 continued to be an eventful year for us. Soon after the experiences described in the previous chapter, my family was vacationing at Windy Hill Beach, SC. We had been pleasantly surprised to learn that Ernest and Dot Welch were staying in the cabin next door. Ernest was now Sunday School Director at Florida Street Baptist in Greensboro, a position I had held before God had thrust me into the ministry seven years earlier. It was Wednesday, August 21, when they came to our door with the news that Tommy Moorefield had been killed in an airplane crash in the Andes Mountains of Brazil. Tommy was one of the first young people to cross our path, one of the "clothesline quarterly" group. He had married Cheryl Smith, also from Florida Street, and they were living in Charleston, SC, where he was stationed with the Air Force. He was co-pilot of the Air Force transport plane at the time of the crash. We later learned that they were active members at Citadel Square Baptist Church where he served as a part-time youth musician. As we later made our way to Greensboro for a memorial service (after days of search, his body was never found), we reflected on the belief that this just couldn't be mere coincidence . . . For at that very time we were talking with a committee from Citadel Square and praying about the possibility of joining their staff!

I continue to be amazed at how God uses all kinds of events to guide us in our walk with Him. It was that same year that a commercial airliner crashed near the Charlotte Airport, bringing tragedy into so many lives. Our pastor was called to assist with the families who were gathering at the airport. As soon as he told me of the crash, I asked, "Where was the plane arriving from?" But somehow I sensed the answer already, "Charleston" . . . It seemed that everywhere I turned, Charleston was before me!

But, lest I leave out part of the story, I must share the background of one other factor that shaped our lives and led us to the inescapable conclusion that God wanted us in Charleston. As a part of the youth section of Vacation Bible School, two years earlier, I had provided training for leadership in Mission Bible Schools. Ten of the group volunteered to hold a mission school in the Fountain Square Apartments Clubhouse. The manager of the apartment community was glad to know we were interested in helping to promote a family emphasis in what had too often been thought of as a "swinging singles" community. There were 454 units in the complex and large numbers of children and teenagers were always gathered around the pool. We were permitted to talk with parents and pre-enroll children at the pool or on the playgrounds. As a result, fifty-one were enrolled and our average attendance was thirty-two per day during that first mission school. Actually, two groups were meeting simultaneously and ten of our high school students provided leadership. They made posters, gathered activity materials, and taught the Bible studies each day. I simply came along to bring refreshments, but, after the first day, some of the girls made brownies and cookies the rest of the week!

We discovered that most of the children were not attending any church on Sundays, so we talked with Charlie Green, who had been using the church bus to pick up about a dozen seniors each Sunday morning. He caught the vision and began making this his last stop each Sunday. This really thrust our church into the bus ministry and they soon added two more busses. Concentrating on apartment areas, within a few months they were making stops in fourteen apartment complexes, and we began holding Children's Church Services for scores of children who had previously been considered "unreachable".

As we talked with children and their parents at Fountain Square, we began to compile a list of teen-agers. The natural question they began to ask as we promoted the Mission Bible School for elementary ages was, "What are you planning to do for us?"

Our list had grown to about fifty as we visited in several homes and asked for names of their friends, so we asked the manager about our beginning a club for teens. To our surprise, he gave me a key and reserved the clubhouse for our use on Thursday nights for a year, and we soon began the "Serendipity Club". Lyman Coleman's *Man Alive* study served as a guide to get us started, and we later turned these weekly sessions into a survey of the Bible. Seven of our older youth, influenced by Ridgecrest experiences and given special training in personal evangelism methods, had opportunities to relate to over a hundred teen-agers during the next two years. The manager not only provided free use of the facilities, but also paid for refreshments every week!

There were many spiritual decisions made during those days, but Ricky Halpern keeps coming to mind. Fourteen years old and the son of Jewish parents who were long-time residents of Fountain Square, Ricky was one of the original members in 1972. After several weeks of studying Old Testament scriptures, he accepted Christ as his Savior and Lord on January 17, 1973. About two months later, he wrote a poem to express his new-found faith. "*Jesus, the Lord*" was later published by *EVENT* magazine (Baptist Sunday School Board, Nashville, Tennessee, March 1974) where it was doubtlessly read by thousands of other youth around the country.

Our experiences at Fountain Square and other apartment communities where we later held Mission Bible Schools, brought me to two firm convictions which have become a part of my ministry over the years. First, apartment complexes are mission fields right at our doorsteps . . . too long we have overlooked these scores of people, while sending our youth on mission trips to pioneer areas. And second, youth become more active through outreach/ministry opportunities than through "fun time" activities centered on themselves. Teen-agers soon become jaded with entertainment programs, but they grow as disciples when they are led to reach out . . . and touch . . . in the name of Christ.

I mentioned earlier that this was a factor in leading us to see that our ministry in Charlotte was about over . . . Almost overnight, for no reason we could understand at the time, attendance at the gatherings at Fountain Square began to dwindle, and it appeared that God was finished with us at that location . . . We came to see sometime later that this was God's way of easing the pain of having to leave these folk we had come to love!

Our Charlotte experiences also confirmed another conviction about youth ministry . . . namely—that more can be accomplished to build relationships through a youth leader's home than will ever be done at the church-house. So many memories crowd in . . . Eddie cutting Rafael's hair, Ronnie asleep on the sofa, Nina and Tinker announcing their engagement, Joyce putting a bead necklace in our mailbox, Don chunking pebbles at our upstairs bedroom window to awaken us and deliver doughnuts at 3:00 a.m.!

This chapter began on a note of sorrow; as I come to the conclusion, another tearful scene comes to mind. As you can well imagine, six years of sharing our lives with so many young people and seeing God at work in and through their lives brought some close ties that were difficult to break. But we were convinced that God wanted us in Charleston, so I resigned as of October 23, 1974 and allowed Him to turn my thoughts and energies toward Citadel Square Baptist Church . . . I could not bear the thought of these young people, almost like a part of our own family, having the feeling that we were deserting them. Nina and Tinker were now married, so we asked them to call together the group at their home. As they sat in a circle around the living room floor, Louise and I explained how God had been working in our lives, too. We told them that I would be reading my resignation at Midwood on Sunday, being fully convinced that this was God's will for us. It was during that experience, amid many tears, that I shared with Frieda my idea for this book. A few days later, we were given a "going away party" and presented a group picture, which we have cherished over the years. What another great surprise when the group came together again on a later evening at Jim and Shirley Stroud's and someone wheeled out a new color TV set. I thought it unusual that we were to watch TV instead of talk, but then someone said, "It's yours . . . to go in your new home!"

In recent years you have seen or heard the quote, "*Life is not measured by the number of breaths we take, but by the moments that take our breath away!*" . . . This was certainly one of those moments! . . . Thank God that tears can never wash away memories!

Fountain Square Bible Study

FOLLOW THAT STAR

Many things had led up to that second trip down Interstate 26 to Charleston . . . the two plane crashes already mentioned, a phone call from Pastor Don Berry just when we had already planned an anniversary trip to Charleston, Don Stroud's unexplained change in their honeymoon plans—to the Isle of Palms instead of Florida, Shirley's dream, the first use of "*Sweet, Sweet Spirit*" at Midwood—a song we had never heard anywhere else except on a Youth Leader's Cruise where we had met Don Berry two years earlier. Louise and I had enjoyed our first Charleston visit, in the penthouse suite at Holiday Inn, just across the street from Citadel Square. And now, we were bringing the children for a visit, this time to meet with the Personnel Committee.

It was late at night and Louise and Tammy were about half asleep in the back seat. Brian and I had been having one of those good father-son chats about school and other teenage concerns. About thirty miles north of Charleston, suddenly I became aware that the sky was completely clouded over, except for one star—straight ahead of us, as if over the city of Charleston! I commented about it to Louise and we agreed that it must be more than coincidence . . . We drove on into the city in almost total silence, reflecting on this strange occurrence. We checked into the Holiday Inn again, and Louise stepped out on the balcony of our penthouse room while I got the suitcases in place. She called me and asked me to look up into the sky—this time in the opposite direction from the time before. There was only one star in sight, and it appeared to be directly above the steeple of the church! I took her hand and said, "I'm ready to move, regardless of what the committee does tomorrow . . ." We went back in the room and got the children in bed. A few minutes later, we walked back out on the balcony, just to meditate on this experience. And as we looked up again, there were stars everywhere—hundreds of them! Now, you're free to interpret that experience however you wish, but I believe God controlled the night sky to give us peace about His purpose for our lives.

We had a good meeting the next day; and as we later drove back up the Interstate toward Charlotte, the song by Jimmy Swaggart from our tape player seemed to take on new meaning, "*There'll Be An Answer By and By . . .*"

AN ALTAR AND A PLOW

After a third trip to Charleston and a week of searching for housing, I begin my work as Minister of Education and Administration at Citadel Square on October 23, 1974, by attending a Stewardship Banquet at Gaillard Auditorium. Other than the shock at the high cost of housing in the area, I was most surprised with the beautiful weather. I remember well a phone call I made to Louise and the children who had stayed in Charlotte until the movers had finished packing. I told them, "It's like being on summer vacation down here every day!" I drove back to Charlotte later that week, and we all came down to our new home on the weekend, just in time to join the church on Louise's birthday, October 27!

During our six years in Charlotte I had completed seminary training, received my Religious Education Certificate, and been licensed by the Midwood Church. It was understood as a part of our call to Citadel Square that I would be ordained in the months that followed. An ordination service was later planned for January 26, 1975, four months after our arrival. I was asked to share some of the mileposts along my spiritual journey as a part of that service. How surprised Louise and I were to have a van-load of young people make the trip from Charlotte to share with us in this special occasion!

It was a meaningful service also because my father was asked to lead the ordination prayer. I'll never forget his voice breaking from the emotion of that moment, and the tender clasp of Louise's hand in mine as I knelt for the traditional "laying-on of hands" ceremony. Pastor Don Berry then spoke to all of us on "*The Paradox of the Altar and the Plow*" using Matthew 2:29 as a text . . . "*Take my yoke upon you and learn of me, for my yoke is easy, and my burden is light.*" He pointed out that our worship should result in work . . . there are needs all around us and we must be willing to take His yoke upon us and go wherever He leads . . . to meet those particular needs He has uniquely equipped us to fill. We must ever keep these symbols before us; they go hand in hand. Worship without work is empty; work without worship is futile.

There are needs all over the world, but I thank God He has counted Louise and me worthy to have met some needs of His children in Charleston!

A Very Special Day

SUMMER HEAT AND WARM FUZZIES

I conducted my first wedding service on July 10 in the prayer room at Citadel Square (I had assisted in the Charlotte weddings of Mary Allen/Rodney Evans and Jan Swett/Don Stroud during the previous year, but I had not performed a ceremony alone since I was not ordained at that time). Leo Hatley, a "young" man at age sixty-six, stopped by our church on the afternoon of July 9. I was the only ministerial staff person present that week, so he shared with me his desire to be married on the following day. It seemed he had met his bride-to-be while they were on a Mediterranean cruise some months before. Margaret Miller, age sixty-five, was from Conway and they had planned to spend their honeymoon in Charleston. He had made the trip from North Myrtle Beach and already reserved a room at the nearby Holiday Inn. This was a second marriage for both, each having outlived their earlier spouses.

We agreed upon a time and I arranged for two secretaries to join us for the ceremony. They came in like two excited teen-agers, with Margaret wearing a beautiful corsage and sporting a dazzling ring the size of which I've never seen on a bride's finger before or since! I thank God He allowed me to be a small part of their happiness on that day.

That same prayer room was the scene of another wedding in April of 1976, as God joined together Matt Jaremko and my secretary, Linden Baker—both in their twenties. Theirs was the most free-form service I've ever conducted, as they had prepared no vows in advance. At the proper time in the ceremony, they simply shared what they were feeling in their hearts. How sweet it was to hear them express their love and commitment to each other in words that came from deep in their hearts, rather than from the lips of a minister! . . . Every wedding which I have conducted becomes very special to me, but the similarities of these two, with couples of such vastly different ages, have made their indelible mark in my memory.

The summer of 1975 also posed another "first" for us. We learned that Citadel Square was so large that it had sufficient numbers of young people to have their own private Youth Camp. In fact, they had been doing so for twenty-five years! Louise and I were asked to be a part of the faculty for the 26th annual assembly—to be held in late July at Camp Forest, a state park near Cheraw, SC. Over one hundred youth attended that week of study, worship, and recreation built around the theme, "*One World; One Lord; One Witness*".

Seasoned "veterans" of previous years gave us one bit of practical advice—"take the biggest fan you can find or better yet, you may want to rent an air conditioner!" . . . Well, when they loaded that U-Haul truck with all the supplies and luggage, I knew we had made our first mistake, for the Pastor and Minister of Music had rented air conditioners! It was too late now, so we "sweated it out" with our too-small fan for a week in the hottest place I've ever been on this earth! Needless to say, an air conditioner had top priority on our packing list in subsequent years. But, even in spite of the heat, and the rusty water that turned iced tea black, and our skin feeling slippery after taking a shower, we had a great week.

My assignment was to teach two identical sessions per day (to two different age groups) on the theme, "*Experiencing the Joy of Koinonia*". Most of those present had never heard the word, "koinonia", which is Greek for "Christian fellowship". Each group spent a total of six hours that week in activities that brought out the real meaning of sharing with one another in the spirit of Christian unity and fellowship. We were deeply touched as the groups showered each other with symbolic gifts after hearing the legendary story of the "Warm Fuzzies". We learned that "cold pricklies" are those words or actions that hurt or offend others; while "warm fuzzies" are those word or actions that affirm others, making them feel wanted and loved. To illustrate the story and make its truth more vivid, I had used little balls of steel wool for "cold pricklies", and cotton balls for "warm fuzzies". And, on the night of our camp report service after returning home, there were tears in many eyes as those youth presented cotton balls to people in the congregation who were special to them—while I told the story of the "*Warm Fuzzies*". My family later presented me with a framed "warm fuzzy"—a large green ball of yarn mounted in a shallow basket for a frame. It became one of our cherished keepsakes.

How about you?—Isn't there someone who would be blessed by a "warm fuzzy" from you today?—A smile, a word of encouragement, an arm around their shoulder, a "cup of cold water" in the name of Christ? . . . They're out there . . . waiting . . .

REAL LOVE AND REALLY LIVING

Not only did we celebrate our nation's Bicentennial in July of 1976, but that same month found us again with a large group of youth at Camp Forest. Louise and I had learned our lesson well during the previous summer, so this time we were armed with a borrowed window air conditioner and several gallons of drinking water "from home"! Camping is OK for Boy Scouts, but give me a few of the comforts of home any day!

We stayed in the "big house" that at least had a bath on the hall—rusty water and all! We never did get bold enough to stay in one of the cabin areas with its community bath consisting of a water hose mounted over an enclosure and connected inside a bucket filled with holes—presto . . . a homemade shower!

Through the years the four cabin areas had been divided between boys and girls on the basis of a small creek that separated "London" and "Paris" from "Honolulu" and "Tokyo". How about those names! They had to do *something* to create excitement in camp. The creek was the absolute dividing line beyond which no boys could go . . . except on arrival day when they helped unload the girl's luggage. But the one bridge that crossed the creek became a popular place after the closing lakeside service each night. So much so that an adult "bridge patrol" had to be assigned to send the lingering ones on to their cabins! This operation became the object of many jokes and a lot of good-natured kidding every week.

The '76 theme was "Living the Christ Life" and my assignment was to lead sessions each day on "*AGAPE: Christian Lifestyle*". Louise led the "morning watch", and her creative lakeside devotionals helped us establish the mood for later studies each day. Our evenings included worship services led by Rev. Joe Weber, camp pastor, and a former "camper" himself. I was particularly intrigued by his choice of sermon titles which had such "youth appeal" . . . "Let Go the Branch", "Shouts in the Night", "Don't Straddle the Fence", etc. I must confess I've used some of his outlines in other settings since that week!

It seemed that the Holy Spirit blended all of the activities of this week together in an unusual way; and we not only learned about a Christian Lifestyle—we lived it!

ARE YOU MY BROTHER?

"*Recognizing Relationships*" became the theme of our 1977 Youth Camp, again held at Camp Forest. Some sixty-five young people devoted a week to a study of the problems encountered by the first family in the Bible and their implications for us. As we looked again at Cain's impertinence as he dared to reply to God, "Am I my brother's keeper?" we struggled to deal with that same question in our lives. We had many activities designed to help us understand both freedom and responsibility, as well as discovering some healthy ways of dealing with anger. Developing a proper self-image, making right choices, being a friend as well as wanting friendship, and guarding against becoming part of a clique, were other important subjects for discussion.

Louise led the "Sonshine Time" (morning watch) each day as we gathered on the banks of Lake Marion just as the sun began to appear over the horizon. Among other resources about relating to each other, she used much of the material from *Being Me* by Grady Nutt (Broadman Press, Nashville, TN, 1971) His words on the subject of patience in relating to others express far more eloquently than I ever could the philosophy Louise and I have tried to follow in ministering to youth through the years . . . "Mushrooms grow to maturity overnight; orchids take seven to twelve years to bloom. Your relationships can be mushrooms or orchids . . . The mature person waits for orchids but is patient with mushrooms!"

We all know that effective learning experiences often are the result of the things that happen to us rather than the things we have merely heard. This week was no exception. Our daughter, Tammy, attended the camp as a true "camper" this year for the first time. Always before she had been required to stay with "Mom and Dad" in the "big house", but now she was old enough to stay in one of the cabins—a new experience for all three of us! Knowing her tendency toward mischief, coupled with her boundless energy, Louise and I were more than a little concerned about what she might "get into" during these long, hot days of summer. But to our surprise, it was our son, Brian, who was involved in an incident that became the talk of the camp that week!

Brian was usually in the right place at the right time, but this occasion was an exception . . . He and four other fellows had conducted a "cabin raid" as they crossed over into one of the girl's areas during afternoon recreation time. Finding the area empty, they overturned suitcases, spilling their contents over the girl's beds. They strewed pine needles all over the floor, scattered debris all over the porch and path leading to the cabin, and found all kinds of ways to use shaving cream inside the cabin itself. Needless to say, the camp pastor had some "counseling sessions" with a captive group of five campers before the week was out. And we had a real-life object lesson to provoke further study about our relationships with each other.

An interesting footnote to this occurrence was that the pastor's daughter later turned a water hose at full pressure into an occupied rest room, but that event was never mentioned publicly . . . Causes one to wonder, what has "Women's Lib" done to us?!

SOMETHING OLD, SOMETHING NEW

A study of relationships was again the theme for our Church Camp in 1978. Our Bible study time was based on the Youth VBS curriculum material "*Something Old; Something New*". We took an in-depth look at the covenant relationship between God and man in the Old Testament and then examined our own relationship with Him and with each other as we explored several New Testament passages. After being exposed to activity-type teaching during previous years, I felt the group entered into the learning activities with more excitement and really gained more from this week-long study. Toward the end of the week, one of the activity groups wrote a song, "*Friends Forever*", which was later published by *EVENT* magazine. Sung to the tune of "*Amazing Grace*", this song became our theme song for the remainder of the week and just watching their facial expressions and hearing them sing it proved that our Bible study had "come alive"!

The following year Louise and I faced "something new", for 1979 marked a turning point in our ministry. Previously Louise and I had led dozens of retreats, Bible studies, etc. for teenagers. But now for the first time we were approached by the Singles class of Citadel Square and asked to lead one of their weekend retreats. The Singles department had grown both numerically and spiritually, and was now holding a weekly home Bible study led by one of their own number—Jim Underhill, a lieutenant commander in the submarine service, stationed at the Charleston Naval Base. The group made all the arrangements concerning food and lodging, and then asked Louise and me to lead them in a study of spiritual gifts. They had rented two cottages on the waterfront at Santee State Park, a beautiful place to grow closer to God and each other as we enjoyed the solitude amidst the wonders of His creation.

We were led to use "*Body Life*" by Ray Steadman as a resource for the study sessions over that weekend and planned a number of activities for personal involvement as we pursued the assigned topic. We were somewhat surprised to find that these single young men and women, all pursuing various directions in their personal careers, developed such a sense of Christian community in only a few brief hours. There were many counseling opportunities, and we concluded the weekend with a determination to devote more time to singles ministry. During the two years that followed, we had the privilege of guiding this ever-expanding group in studies on "How to Find and Follow God's Will", "Discovering and Using Your Spiritual Gifts", as well as participating with them in regular Bible studies each Friday night. We also found ourselves involved in pre-marital conferences with several of them and saw God bring five couples to the marriage altar. We have maintained a special closeness to John and Cammie Steele, and were honored to assist in John's ordination after they returned from three years in seminary.

As we became more aware of young marrieds and their needs, we had opportunity to lead two retreats for married couples dealing with "Communication in Marriage". Our own marriage has been strengthened through the years as God has opened doors to new areas of service . . . teaching *us* in the process!

EXISTENCE, ENDURANCE, OR EXCITEMENT

The decade of the Eighties began for us with a traumatic year and brought many changes in our lives. Our pastor had resigned in August of 1977 after seven years of trying to overcome "church politics" in a traditional old inner-city church. The open struggle between the "pioneers" and the "settlers" finally became so intense that he had no other choice. Against the advice of many of my colleagues around the convention, I remained as the only full-time member of the ministerial staff through the fifteen months the church was without a pastor.

A new pastor came in December 1978, followed shortly thereafter by a minister to Youth and College ages. Another eighteen months passed, with slight gains noted in Sunday School enrollment amid continued polarization of the church membership. The leadership "power structure" quickly shifted back to the older members in the congregation, and singles and young couples grew more disenchanted.

In the midst of this unsettled environment, Louise and I celebrated our 25th wedding anniversary! Our church bookkeeper had resigned after her husband's death, and had opened a travel agency in North Charleston. She made all the arrangements for us to fly to Hawaii and spend eight days in Waikiki which included a tour of some of the major attractions on Oahu. We flew to Chicago and then boarded a non-stop flight to Honolulu. Prior to our leaving, some ladies in the church arranged a reception in our honor, and some of our friends had included cash gifts in their cards of congratulations, so I used these funds to buy dozens of rolls of camera film. I had bought a new camera for the trip and planned to have plenty of pictures when we returned. It was June of 1980 and our flight plan took us very near Mount St. Helens, which had erupted a short time before. When we were approaching it, the pilot came on the speaker and said, "I will tilt the wing down so you can see it out the right side of the plane." I had been snapping pictures of O'Hare airport and the cloud formations along the way, so now I snapped several of the smoke still rising down below. Later, I did the same at Honolulu airport and captured scenes from the bus on the way to our hotel. Imagine how disappointed I was when we arrived in our room and I started to reload the camera, only to find it didn't have any film in it! The excitement of the reception and anticipation of our trip had completely caused me to forget to put film in the camera!

Well, I made up for it the rest of the week . . . We had almost 400 pictures developed upon our return. While we were in Hawaii, our tour took us to Punchbowl Cemetery, Ernie Pyle's grave site, the Arizona Memorial at Pearl Harbor, the house where Robert Louis Stevenson lived when he wrote *The Little Grass Shack*, etc. We also were able to see the annual King Kamahamaha Parade in person and get scores of pictures of the beautiful flowers adorning the many horses and floats that day. In fact, about half the passengers on our plane flight were teenagers from a high school in Indiana whose band had been invited to march in the parade.

On another occasion we struck out on our own to ride a bus to the Dole Pineapple factory. At that time you could ride a bus anywhere on the island for fifty cents and transfer to a different bus at no charge! The bus was crowded and we had to sit separately in the only seats available. I was sitting beside a beautiful Hawaiian girl and her question about the shiny new diamond ring Louise had given me afforded an opportunity to share that we were celebrating 25 years! I then asked Louise to turn and show her the new one I had given her also. This seemed a good time to ask if I might take the Hawaiian girl's picture, and when she agreed, I stood to get a better angle with my camera. At about that same time, the driver announced our stop and Louise exited through the rear doors of the bus, thinking I was right behind her. To my surprise the driver pulled away, leaving me still on the bus! Fortunately the next stop was only one block away, so I was able to get off and run back to the street corner where Louise was standing in bewilderment. It turned out that the young girl got off the bus at that same stop but I was so flustered that I didn't think to ask her to pose for a better picture. We've laughed about this for years, but at the time Louise didn't think it was a bit funny!

After the first few days, we then phoned a couple of former church members who had moved back to Oahu from Citadel Square some months before. His father was in the Air Force and had previously been stationed in Hawaii where both sons married Hawaiian girls. When he was transferred to the Charleston Air Force Base, both new couples moved also, and they all had joined Citadel Square. The other couple found their "niche" and adjusted to living in South Carolina, but this couple had moved back to Kaneohe to be near the wife's parents. So, when we called, they insisted that we let them pick us up and take us to see some other parts of the island. The rest of the week we spent together, allowing us to see a lot of scenery we would have missed otherwise. He was a teacher at Hawaii Baptist Academy and she played piano for a Baptist church where we attended on Sunday. While visiting a public park on the back side of Oahu, we came upon a scene that called to mind what the garden in Eden must have looked like. I tried to capture it on camera but you would have had to be there to experience it fully.

Less than six weeks after our return, in late July of 1980, we packed up again for a week of Sunday school training at Ridgecrest. One day before we were scheduled to leave, I was told by the Personnel Committee, "Our pastor now wants to call his own staff, replacing your position as Minister of Education/Administration with four Division Directors. Since you will be with other folks from around the convention all next week, we would appreciate your beginning to look for another place of service." That statement was followed by expressions of appreciation for my six years among them, that there was really no date in mind, and assurances that they would recommend me to any church in the convention. Years later, those words still sound hollow, when in effect, a church says, "You're doing a great job, and we will recommend you highly, but . . . *we* don't want you any longer!"

I do not agree in any wise with this prerogative of pastors, which relegates other ministerial staff persons to mere *employees*, rather than recognizing God's call both *to* and *away from* a particular place of ministry. Unfortunately, this approach seems to have become far too prevalent in churches over the past several years. However, not wishing to create further tension among the church fellowship, I began the following day to comply with their wishes.

Needless to say, our week at Ridgecrest was a blur of hurt and disappointment since this abrupt approach by the Personnel Committee came as a complete shock, without any hint from the pastor that he was even thinking of such an idea. Louise and I spent much time in the prayer garden, and we were blessed by a two-hour conference with Dr. Adrian Rogers and his wife.

The love and support of this "pastor for the week" was most encouraging, but a poster found at the assembly gift shop also was used by God to touch us just where we needed it most . . .

It pictured a narrow winding road leading to a rainbow and the statement, "The Rocky Road Before You Now . . . May Lead to a Rainbow".

I placed it on the bedroom wall where we could see it often during the week. Our dear friends, Jim and Shirley Stroud, came up from Charlotte for the weekend to share with us during this difficult time. In the weeks that followed, I tried every way I could think of to leave Charleston, feeling that the memory of this painful experience would limit our effectiveness and future ministry unless we physically relocated. We talked with one or more representatives from churches in seven other cities, and visited one church field to meet with a committee, but in every case, God made it so evident that all those doors were closed to us. At the same time, He opened wide a door of opportunity at Fort Johnson Baptist Church on James Island, the first church to contact me after our return from Ridgecrest. I procrastinated . . . No, I guess I actually *argued* with the Lord about staying that close by, but He made it so plain that no other decision would do.

We became part of the Fort Johnson fellowship on October 20, 1980. God was good to us during those early years at Fort Johnson . . . He permitted us to build a house nearby and get out of the rental cycle that we had been in ever since we moved to Charleston. Our work at Fort Johnson did not include working directly with young people, as another staff member was assigned that ministry. The church had an active youth program, primarily centered around music, puppetry, and social activities. They usually made one trip each summer to assist in Mission work—mostly in campgrounds of Gatlinburg or Myrtle Beach. Several Backyard Bible Clubs were held for a week prior to their trip each year and in 1982 they began an annual week of Mission Vacation Bible School among the migrant children on nearby Johns Island.

The church was really located in a mission field with new houses and apartments being built all around the area. We participated in a pilot project sponsored by Ralph Neighbour and West Memorial Baptist of Houston in 1981. "Project 80" was an effort by 80 churches to field-test the use of share groups and TOUCH ministries which had been so successful in reaching "outsiders" in the Houston, area. This approach to evangelism was reaching staggering numbers of unsaved people in Singapore, Korea, South America, and certain parts of the United States.

For several years I also became increasingly more active in Associational work, having served as ASSIST Director for five years and then as "8.5 by '85" Area Representative. It was my privilege to serve one year as Vice-moderator of Charleston Baptist Association and as chairman of their Long-range Planning Committee.

During the first four years we served at Fort Johnson, the pastor and I practiced what I considered "shared ministry". I was Associate Pastor by function, although never officially given that title. We had opportunities that drew us close to many people—especially Milton and Sylvia Ivie and Ted and Annie Laurie Ludwig. Over the six years on their staff, I was called upon to conduct sixteen funerals and privileged to officiate at thirty-eight weddings. Louise directed several of the weddings, which were always celebrations that came together "without a hitch"! . . . I've worked with many wedding directors through the years, which always confirms what I already know—that my wife is the best in the business!

But, good things always seem to come to an end . . . The pastor resigned in the fall of 1984, and again we stayed through eight months without a pastor. At the request of the Personnel Committee and Deacons, I managed the administrative affairs and pastoral care needs while supply preachers were called in on Sundays. In June of 1985 they called a twenty-eight-year old as pastor whose approach to ministry was totally opposite from mine. I'm sure our age difference was a contributing factor (our own son was twenty-six at the time), but our philosophies of relationships and methods were poles apart! He even said from the pulpit that, "Instead of asking permission, I had rather act and then ask forgiveness later"! This was only his second church position since graduating from seminary, and he had never had experience dealing with a multiple staff situation. There were "behind the scenes" attempts to cause both myself and the Music/Youth minister to leave. Those were difficult days but God is faithful . . . He was preparing another place of service for us, and in October 1986 we joined the staff of Rosewood Baptist Church in Columbia, SC.

Several months after I resigned, there was an open confrontation that resulted in secret ballots related to keeping or dismissing the pastor and/or the music minister. After a three-hour business meeting, this resulted in an ugly church split with some thirty families leaving with the pastor to start a new congregation. Some time later, following their call of a new pastor, the music minister was asked to leave . . . . It's a shame how Satan can get a foothold in a local church and stop the growth of God's work in a community! . . . I'm so thankful we had been "lifted out" of that situation earlier as I have never wanted to be a cause of dissension in a church.

Our 25th Anniversary

MATURE IN YEARS; YOUNG AT HEART

Our move to Columbia meant leaving our son, Brian, and his family behind. He had graduated from College of Charleston and begun work in the accounting department of a family owned firm where he later became Comptroller and a Vice-president. After twenty-three years, the company was bought out by a Texas conglomerate and he had to seek other employment. He still lives on James Island where he has bought a house and is employed as Finance Manager for a large manufacturing firm in North Charleston. Our daughter, Tamela, had moved some time earlier to Virginia when her husband was transferred by the Navy to the Virginia Beach area. After receiving training and licensing in the mental health field, she now lives in Roanoke, VA and is employed by a private firm that provides resources and group homes for mentally challenged adults in the Salem, VA area. So, unlike our move with two children twelve years earlier, this time it was just the two of us making our way to a new field of service!

Rosewood Baptist was made up mostly of Senior Adults and Singles. We had opportunity to work with both . . . A new Singles Sunday School Department had been formed the year before we came, but seemed to have reached a plateau with about a dozen in attendance. After consultation with the department leadership, we decided to try a new approach . . . Ten "facilitators" were enlisted and we began using the "master teacher" concept with Ralph Neighbors' videotaped LIFE Basic Training Series. After showing a fifteen-minute segment each Sunday, we divided into five sharing groups for discussion and application. Using this approach, the attendance *doubled* in only three months!

During 1987-88, Rosewood was asked to serve as a pilot church for introducing LIFE courses by the Baptist Sunday School Board. We used the Singles Department to launch our own "Lay Institute for

Equipping" as we used "*Master Design: an Inductive Study of Ephesians*" to follow up the LIFE Basic Training.

From the day we first arrived at Rosewood, the Senior Adults loved and encouraged us in so many ways. During those years, we entered their ranks in terms of chronological age and soon felt right at home at the "Retirees' Breakfast" and their monthly "Young at Hearts" luncheon meeting. Louise and I were asked several times to be the featured speaker at each of those groups. It was a joy to see their eyes light up when we walked into the room. There were so many of them who had learned the secret of being "Young at Heart"—and age makes no difference! It has been our privilege in the years since to maintain social contacts with many of them, and I have been called upon to officiate at both weddings and funerals in the group! In fact, some years later, we were part of a group of ten who flew to Honolulu and boarded the S.S. Independence, where we lived for a week and enjoyed five ports of call around the Hawaiian Islands. We had made our plans to arrive one day earlier, so after checking into our hotel for the night, we got together to decide where to eat that evening. The group finally decided to board a bus and ride into downtown Honolulu in search of a restaurant. Would you believe, with all the choices of unique native food, we ended up at a Red Lobster . . . a chain that we had frequented so many times in Columbia! We did later enjoy a real Luau and outdoor stage show at sunset held on the premises of the Sheraton Resort on the island of Maui! There were several other memorable events on that trip, including being signed up without our knowledge to play in a Newlyweds Game aboard ship, and being so tired out during a long layover in Dallas/Ft. Worth on our return that Louise and I laid down on the floor of the airport for a nap! That resulted in several pictures and brought a lot of laughs after we returned home.

Mother's Day, 1990 . . . Here we go again! Shortly after his fifth anniversary at Rosewood, the pastor resigned and left for a church in Wilmington, NC. Since this was the third time we had experienced this situation in our many years of ministry, we knew the future months would be difficult. Someday I'm going to ask the Lord why we were called upon to stay behind and help "hold things together" while a church went through these transition times. We know someone is needed to provide some sense of stability in the church, but it was always an unsettling time for us personally . . .

September arrived and we found ourselves on vacation at Crescent Beach, SC. It had been a traumatic summer . . . We saw a five per cent gain in Sunday School and Discipleship Training attendance over 1989, rather than having the traditional "summer slump". Yet, during the same time, rumors began to circulate regarding the remaining staff. It seemed that one man in the church, who had become adept at "church politics" and somehow had come to hold *eight* major leadership positions, had expressed that, "We need a clean slate; all our staff should leave before we call a new pastor." Essentially this was the view of our former pastor, although he gave a different reason. He expressed to me on his last day in the office, "This church doesn't deserve you; you need to just devote all your time to finding another place of service!" . . . From his perspective, that may have sounded OK, but then, who would have held the seven funerals I was called upon to officiate during those succeeding months? I was even more firmly convinced that God called me to the gospel ministry first—and to me that means meeting human needs! He secondarily has provided the avenue of Religious Education as a specialty and has gifted me with skills in administration and teaching.

It's a fine line to walk—to respond to pastoral ministry needs, without being looked upon as a threat to any future pastor. I could not turn my back on people I had come to love in the past four years, until God told *me,* "It's enough", and called me to another field of service or released me from His call to this particular congregation.

This had been my philosophy for over twenty-five years and remains so until this day. However, churches have changed a great deal from what they were in 1967 when God first called us into the ministry. "Church politics" have become the order of the day, and few churches have escaped the division that comes about when members lose sight of God as the head of His church and decide to run things themselves. I fear the Lord has left many of them to their own devices, and they are being destroyed from within.

Although the Deacon body soundly rejected the idea of a "clean slate" at first, this one self-appointed church "savior" began a campaign behind the scenes and "under the table" which made life miserable for all of us. (The Music Minister, Youth Minister, Educational Secretary, Financial Secretary, and Pianist all resigned in the succeeding weeks). I knew what was going on, but refused to confront the issue publicly, as I didn't want to cause division in the church body. It was only after he had enlisted agreement from the Deacon Chairman and the Pastor Search Committee, that he was bold enough to admit his views in a Deacon's meeting. I tried without success to share with the leaders that this was not God's way of doing things. But, after the second meeting, where the minutes of the previous meeting were actually *changed* to reflect entirely different conversations than what had actually taken place, that I realized there was no hope. I had been losing sleep for two weeks or more, and felt I would be of no use physically or emotionally if I didn't get out of the situation.

I resigned publicly on March 17,1991, and attempted to share as tactfully as possible what had been going on behind the scenes, as I still believe 95% of the congregation were unaware why all the staff were leaving. That same weekend, the Receptionist mailed her resignation to the Personnel Committee and the Organist resigned two weeks later. This left only the Custodian in a church with NO other staff! . . . (He was dismissed once a new pastor arrived!) I'm convinced God took His hands off that church as they went through some very painful experiences in the next three or four years . . . eventually culminating in a church split with a disgruntled pastor, after being dismissed in a tumultuous business meeting, taking dozens of members with him and forming a new church!

WHAT *IS* MINISTRY ANYWAY?

I was so emotionally "burned out" after the experiences of the previous chapter, that I prayed for God to give me freedom to pursue other avenues of service outside a local church. I had conversations with various departments at the Baptist State Convention offices, Baptist Hospital, and Connie Maxwell Children's Home. At the same time, I sent out resumes to several businesses for positions for which I felt I was suited. The one door that opened wide was to become involved with Metropolitan Life as a potential Financial Services Representative. I saw this as an opportunity to minister to a large segment of the community that I could never have reached as a church staff member, and determined to make it a *ministry*.

My parents had taken out a small insurance policy on my life with Metropolitan the month I was born, and had given it to me after our marriage. I never dreamed I would be employed by such a large company, but it seemed God blessed my efforts in those initial months of training and I was soon "on my own" in building an agency. During the next several years, I continued to study and attained the coveted industry designations of Certified Life Underwriter and Chartered Financial Consultant. Over time, I was given a large number of client files from departing agents, and I was able to personally add over one hundred new clients to our files in the first year. I concentrated on retired and semi-retired folks and became very involved with investments as well as insurance. My previous experience as a minister served me well, as I had many opportunities to assist widows in filing death claims and handling final details, which were often so unfamiliar to them.

During the years I had served as a church staff member, Louise and I had been able to attend Southern Baptist Convention meetings in New Orleans, Houston and Norfolk, as well as training conferences in Nashville, Memphis, and Detroit. We were now fortunate to be invited, at MetLife's expense, to attend Leadership Conferences held at the Ritz-Carlton Resort in Amelia Island, Florida and at the Broadmoor Resort in Colorado Springs, Colorado. One year we also were treated to a cruise with Royal Caribbean to the Bahamas! We continue to be amazed at the beauty of this world in which we live, and thank God that He has allowed us to have opportunities over the years to travel and experience more of His creation outside our home state of North Carolina.

I began to visit my insurance clients in times of hospitalization and was called upon to officiate at weddings of some of their children. A few have asked, "Why did you leave the ministry?" . . . My reply has been, "I didn't leave the ministry; I just don't look to a church to pay my salary any more!" In many respects I have been freed to meet people's needs, instead of meeting the endless requirements of committee meetings and church gatherings where we only rubbed shoulders with Christian people! . . . And I'd like to think that God also enabled me during those years to improve the image of an "insurance agent" in the eyes of the general public.

During these years in the mid to late Nineties, we had joined Trinity Baptist Church in Cayce, SC, and Louise started teaching a ladies' Sunday school class. A year or so later, a nucleus of three men from the senior men's class joined me in starting a new class for middle-aged men. This age group had been largely overlooked in the structure of the Sunday school, and there were scores of church members in that age bracket who just didn't want to go in the oldest men's class! We both enjoyed these seven or eight years of teaching, without the pressures that come from actually being a paid staff member. During this time, we learned that the house we had bought some years before was located on a street that was soon to become a busy travel route to the Interstate via the new 12th street extension connector. This also meant that our street would be widened and we would lose fifteen feet of our front yard, so we decided it was time to move again! After weeks of house hunting, we found a house in a quiet, suburban part of Lexington and moved there in the spring of 2001. This location was fifteen miles from Trinity Baptist and we soon tired of making thirty mile round-trips to stay active there. We resigned our teaching positions and began to visit many of the churches in Lexington but just couldn't seem to find one that God would give us peace about moving our membership. During this time we actually took the opportunity of worshipping with His people of various denominations around the area and made some new friends we never would have met otherwise.

Financial Services Executive
Larry D. Sledge, CLU, ChFC

MINISTRY TAKES MANY FORMS

In June of 2001, when I had completed ten years with MetLife, I decided to go part-time on a retirement contract which gave me more free time to be used wherever God might lead. This retirement contract ended in March of 2006, but I retained my insurance credentials for use with other companies . . .

In March of 2002, I was finally able to convince my Dad, who was becoming more feeble with age, to move into an apartment at Deepwood Estates, an independent living facility just three miles from our home in Lexington, SC. He had been living alone since my mother's death four years earlier in Trinity, NC . . . just a few miles from where I grew up. This allowed me to have some quality time with him for about two months before he required surgery for a blood clot on his brain and subsequently died nine days later from breathing complications. During this time, I became acquainted with the management staff at the facility, and for months after Dad's death I felt a call to begin a Bible study on their premises. I discussed this with the managers and they blocked out a time on Wednesday nights when no other activities were planned. Louise and I began to enjoy dinner with the residents and lead a Bible Book study following the meal each week. After this activity became so well-attended, a new manager asked us to consider holding a worship service in the Chapel each Sunday morning at 11:00. After praying about it, we realized that God had this in mind all along . . . that's why we had not felt led to join a new church since we had moved to Lexington! So, we began this ministry at Easter, 2004, and continue to feel God's blessing on our involvement at Deepwood. Louise's caring spirit and loving actions toward these residents also led them to ask her to serve as "Queen Mother" to a Red Hat Society chapter which meets there once a month. For over seven years now, we have been doing this, as well as continuing the weekly Bible study! . . . This has allowed us to meet many new friends and God has used us to minister to a number of them who become hospitalized or are facing changes in their lives. It's been a blessing to serve as sort of an unofficial "chaplain" to this group from various faiths. I have also been called upon to conduct several memorial services for residents who have passed away during these years.

In June of 2005, we were so blessed to be able to celebrate our 50th wedding anniversary!

Even though we were no longer attending there, except for an occasional evening service, our friends at Trinity Baptist allowed us to use their fellowship building to hold a reception. Louise prepared much of the food, I assembled a large "strawberry tree" using fresh strawberries, and some friends helped with decorations. Our son, Brian, set up a camera to take a separate photo of each couple or individual who attended, and we took dozens of pictures of the food and decorations. Scores of our friends from churches and/or work places came to enjoy an evening of great fun and fellowship. We were especially touched by many who came from North Carolina to celebrate and reminisce with us! That same week, we were privileged to celebrate with a cruise to the Caribbean with stops that included Montego Bay, Jamaica, and Cozumel, Mexico.

As I complete the final chapter of this book that has been in process over many years, we have just celebrated our 56th anniversary with a cruise to the Bahamas!

We are still staying busy during our retirement years, and, looking back, I am so glad God has allowed us to cross paths with so many of His children . . . many of whom have left "footprints on our hearts"! I'm also grateful that the truths of three favorite scriptures have become true in my life by experience:

> *"I have learned, in whatsoever state I am, therewith to be content."*—Philippians 4:11
>
> *"I can do all things through Christ who strengtheneth me."*—Philippians 4:13
>
> *"And we know that all things work together for good to them that love God; to them who are called according to his purpose"*—Romans 8:28

Most of all, we'll always be thankful for each of the young people mentioned in the earlier chapters of this book . . . They have truly helped our lives to be "Fun in the Son!"

Our 50th Anniversary

Deepwood Estates

EPILOGUE

This is not the end . . . only a *way-station* in our Christian pilgrimage. We're living in the so-called "retirement years", but God isn't finished with any of us yet. He not only wants us to *bloom where we are planted*, but to be different from every other flower in His garden. Your experiences will not be the same as ours, but I trust that the words on these pages have encouraged you in your Christian walk . . . challenged you to love others along the way . . . or pointed you to the Son who stands ready to walk with all of us into the future! May you also experience *FUN in the SON* and stay "young" all the days of your life!

Larry Sledge
June, 2011

We've Only Just Begun!

FRIENDS FOREVER

(Sing to the tune of "Amazing Grace")

How much our friendship means to me,
I know it will not end.
It lifts me up when I am down,
For you're my dearest friend.

When times are hard, you're always there,
To talk our problems through.
We share our dreams, our hopes, our fears,
I've found a friend in you!

(Written by the youth of Citadel Square Baptist Church, Charleston, SC, and published in *EVENT* magazine, Baptist Sunday School Board, Nashville, Tennessee, August, 1980)

FLORIDA STREET YOUTH

Alexander, Tony
Baker, Roger
Baker, Wayne
Bennett, Jerry
Billings, Eddie
Brooks, Susan
Buckner, Ronnie
Buckner, Susan
Carratello, Phyllis
Carter, Karen
Culbreth, Shirley
Dalche, David
Darnell, Jane
Deaton, Joe
Deaton, Pat
Frazier, Brenda
Glass, Linda
Hinson, Lee
Holmes, Wayne
Howell, Charles
Huckabee, Deanna
Hughes, Anna Ruth
Lefler, Fonda
Lohr, Dottie
Loftis, Lydia
Martin, Billie Kay
Miller, David
Miller, Donna
Moorefield, Charlie
Moorefield, Tommy
Newnam, Eddie
O'Ferrell, Gail
Parrish, Sarah
Phelps, Carol
Phelps, Jennifer
Pickard, Pam

Pope, Jimmy
Pope, Pat
Poplin, Wayne
Rachol, Luther
Reams, David
Rumbley, Lea
Schenk, Becky
Shore, Phyllis
Simmons, Phil
Sizemore, Patsy
Smith, Cheryl
Stamey, Jimmy
Stanley, "Skipper"
Welch, Donnie
Wilder, Brenda
Wilder, Diane

BESSEMER YOUTH

Bethea, Johnny
Blake, Carla
Cox, Bonnie
Cox, Diane
Dowd, David
Green, H.D.
Paschal, Pat
Sewell, Carolyn
Sewell, Teresa
Stevens, Debbie
Umfleet, Donna
Underwood, Ken
Wallen, Jimmy
Ward, Ginny
Ward, Jimmy

MIDWOOD YOUTH—SENIOR HIGH or older

Airey, George
Airey, Larry
Allen, Mary
Anderson, Lee
Bass, Joyce
Bell, Connie
Blanton, Shelly
Burns, Herbie
Campbell, Bobby
Campbell, Mike
Chambers, Clifton
Clemons, Ruth
Collins, Mitchell
Collins, Robert
Collins, Rocky
Cook, Chip
Cook, Randy
Cotton, Ricky
Cranford, Jeff
Danner, Linda
Davenport, Rebecca
Davis, Eddie
Davis, Phil
Edwards, Freda
Evans, Rodney
Fadel, Kim
Flowers, Debbie
Fryes, Carla
Gardner, Mary Susan
Gonzalez, Rafael
Greene, Lewis
Haga, Patricia
Hands, Dennis
Harris, Don
Hattrich, Neal
Helms, Dianne

Henderson, Martha
High, Alysia
Holloway, David
Holloway, Emil
Hoover, Perrie
Kinard, Herbert
King, Pam
Kissiah, Marilyn
Lawter, Suzanne
Lewis, Stephen Henry
Lloyd, Joyce Ann
Loftis, Frieda
Long, Niles
Long, Renee
Love, Jamie
Martin, Patsy
Maynor, Gail
McGuinn, Marshall
McHenry, Debbie
McIntyre, Pam
McWhirter, Janice
Medlin, Michael
Moffitt, Sheila
Monroe, Steve
Morgan, Charles
Morris, Ricky
Mullis, Charles
Mullis, Patsy
Nealy, Michael
Norris, Linda
Outlaw, "Tinker"
Patton, Lori
Phillips, Betty Ann
Phillips, Ron
Privett, Mike
Queen, Debra
Rhodes, Pamela
Rhodes, Tommy

Scofield, Pat
Self, David
Self, Lane
Shaver, Billy
Sherrill, Bobby
Smith, Beverly
Snyder, Susan
Starnes, Kay
Steed, Rodger
Steinback, Debby
Stroud, Don
Sullivan, James
Sullivan, Penny
Sutherland, Debbie
Tadlock, Carlton
Tadlock, Cheri
Walker, Debbie
Wall, Pat
White, Phyllis
Williams, Harry
Williams, Larry
Willis, Laura
Willis, Merilyn
Worrell, Kemp
Wyatt, Kim
Wyatt, Nina
Young, Billy

JUNIOR HIGH

Bentley, Jeff
Brewer, Joel
Brewer, Terri
Campbell, Jimmy
Christie, Pat
Conder, Donald
Conder, Ronald
Cook, Nina
Cook, Randy
Cranford, Jeff
Crawley, Cynthia
Crawley, Elizabeth
Detter, Mike
Elam, Jo
Everidge, Rhonda
Freeman, John
Frick, David
Fuller, Susan
Gaddis, Ann
Godfrey, Karen
Greene, Diane
Hands, Diane
Hands, Steven
Harrington, Douglas
Harrington, Judy
Helms, Keith
Henderson, Eddie
Henderson, Patty
Holloway, Delene
Holloway, John
Hudgins, Stuart
Jones, Ronnie
Lewis, Ben
Lloyd, Don
Lloyd, Pamela Merice
Loftis, Joyce

Long, Renee
Medlin, Keith
Monroe, Donna
Nealy, James
Norris, David
Nunn, Gay
Pait, Barbara
Pate, Jack Lee
Patton, Keith
Pearce, Cathie
Perry, Ann
Phillips, Alec
Privett, Steve
Rallis, Chris
Riggins, Randy
Ross, Beverly
Scofield, Steve
Sellers, Teresa
Shaver, Maria
Shelton, Ted
Smith, Joan Annette
Smith, Mike
Smith, Steve
Steed, Billy
Stevens, Ronnie
Sullivan, Clyde
Sullivan, Terry
Sullivan Eddie
Talbert, Patricia
Teal, Mark
Toney, Patti
Trexler, Chip
Wall, Anne
Willis, Kathy
Wilson, Phillip
Wyatt, Regina
Zink, Robin

FOUNTAIN SQUARE YOUTH SERENDIPITY CLUB

Cheryl Boutet
Michael Boutet
Denise Brunt
Lisa Brunt
Lori Brunt
Russell Brunt
Kevin Davis
Mike Davis
Tony Frais
Joey Frais
Ricky Furr
Jeff Goble
Steve Grant
Elizabeth Griffith
Jeff Halpern
Ricky Halpern
Chris Harrington
Eddie Helms
E.R. Jarvis
Cassady Laizure
David Lee
Robin Lee
Gary LeFew
Susan Markley
Donna McDaniel
Patty McDaniel
Cliff McFarland
Courtney McFarland
Tommy McFarland
Scott McLeod
Chris Meadows
Mike Murray
Jackie Overcash
Scott Pressley
Debbie Pressley

Pam Pressley
Ricky Ross
Tina Ross
Sue Scaife
Rita Scaife
Billy Smith
Patty Smith
Joel Speller
Lydia Sykes
Julie Tarleton
Kim Tarleton
Sue Tighe
Barry Turner
Cindy Turner
Randy Turner
Debra Wilkes
Cathy Williams